The Art of Colonial Flower Arranging

The Art of
Colonial Flower
Arranging

Jean C. Clark

The Pyne Press
Princeton

*Library of Congress Catalog Card Number
73-75214
SBN 87861-045-6*

*Jacket design by Lance Hiddy
Drawings by Gwendolyn O. England
Photographs by Froehlich Studio
Book design by Robert Reed
Manufactured in the
United States
of America*

For Juliet Bloor

Note of Acknowledgment

Special thanks are due to several persons who have provided valuable information and assistance: Christel Ruehle, Virginia Armstrong, Kit Callender, and Beatrice Heermance.

For the determined and skillful ministrations of Betty Davison, I am most appreciative and admiring.

Jean Clark
Princeton
May 13, 1974

Contents

Harmonious Bouquets

Classic Simplicity

The Art of Colonial Flower Arranging

I

A Personal Adventure

IT SEEMED SIMPLE ENOUGH at the time. The call had come to me from Mrs. Agnes Hoke, who said she needed temporary help in sorting some dried flowers she had grown or collected from the fields around Princeton, New Jersey. No special talent was required, she said. A sense of color and the ability to identify the fifteen or sixteen different plant materials she included in her boxes of "natural color dried flowers" would be adequate preparation for the job. The best part of the offer seemed to be that I could work on whatever schedule I chose. That meant that I could sort flowers while the girls were in school and be home when they returned, and in time for my afternoon piano students. So off I went to Mrs. Hoke's loft, where the rafters were almost totally obscured by bunches of goldenrod and dock that were being hang dried.

That was back in 1957, the day after Mrs. Hoke had received a deparment-store order for one hundred boxes of her assorted flowers. These had, until then, been sold only in the local gift shop. Seventeen years later, I find myself a partner, with Elizabeth Flanders and Barbara Platten, in a business known as Eighteenth Century Bouquet, Inc.

Clearly, Agnes Hoke's job description had been somewhat inaccurate. This pianist and music teacher rapidly became addicted to dried plant materials and to making arrangements in the eighteenth century manner. Many were the nights I went back to the loft to watch Agnes at work or to do over one of my own arrangements that she had found wanting.

Working with flowers and being oriented toward the colonial period were not totally alien interests, however. Some years before all of this my family and I had moved into an old farmhouse on a commercial flower farm—with six acres of peonies and innumerable lilac bushes. Until the prices dropped so much as to make it unprofitable, the whole family cooperated in the process of getting sixty dozen peonies and fifty bunches of lilacs to the New York flower market by three o'clock in the morning during the season. Even the girls, not yet in their teens, helped with the picking and bundling. And the barns, where we prepared the flowers and kept them until time to go to market, must have been

1

the sweetest smelling anywhere. During the rest of the year much of my time was spent in trying to restore the old farmhouse and scouting the countryside for the kind of furnishings its original owners had probably had. Because of that, the posy holders, Franklin urns, and delft bricks that Agnes used for her arrangements seemed somehow familiar.

Eventually Agnes moved away, but fortunately only after she had passed on her enthusiasm for Colonial Williamsburg, where she had worked for many years, and particularly for Louise Fisher's eighteenth century arrangements that for so long decorated the official buildings there. During many of those years, Agnes had been responsible for the arangements at the Williamsburg Inn, and it was then that she became intrigued with the possibility of introducing more natural color into winter bouquets. The years between her work at Williamsburg and the opening of her dried flower business in Princeton were spent in experimenting with ways to preserve the more delicate flowers in blues and pinks and reds. The colonists had loved these in summer bouquets but, until they began dying everlastings, use of such colors was denied during the cold and bleak winter.

Agnes taught me more than the art of arranging flowers in the eighteenth century manner. It was from her that I learned how to walk in the woods with my eyes really open. It was marvelous to discover that the paths I had known for years were suddenly full of fascinating shapes and colors and that it was fun to experiment with different methods of preserving their beauty. Now, even after years of exploring and plant collecting, Princeton still holds wonderful surprises for me. While picking goldenrod near the local airport just this past fall, I happened on a plant whose stems bear lots of fascinating tiny pointed pods. Unfortunately, a botanist friend told me that the plant's identity could not be determined until next summer; it was too late to get a sample of its leaves. In the meantime, I call it "airport weed."*

It took a bit of experimenting before it could be included in arrangements, however. A few days after I had delivered my great discovery to the shop and everyone had exclaimed over its beauty, we began to notice a rather strange odor. Some of my less sympathetic colleagues changed its name to "stink weed" for a while. Eventually, we found that coating the branches with clear floral spray made it a welcome addition to our storehouse. Since we had never before found a plant with anything like that interesting growth pattern and delicate pod, we plan to be frequent airport visitors. Unless it is an endangered plant, I feel sure the management will be cooperative. And now we have a new excuse for hikes in the area.

I remember one time when my husband, Frank, consented to my going on a "hike" with him, his friend Glenn, and Holly, the dog, while they hunted for pheasants. After a couple of hours, I came upon a huge patch of fuzzy beige grass growing against an old farm fence and began

---

*We have since learned that it is hairy beard-tongue.

to gather as much as I could carry. When Glenn saw what I was doing, he decided to pick some too. There were no pheasants anyway. Two armfuls of lovely field grass were the "game" of the day.

Although most of my "flower time" is now spent in arranging, I still go plant hunting as often as possible on my own or with anyone I can corral and spend every spare moment collecting loosestrife, Queen Anne's lace, early and late goldenrod, and dock in its three different and useful stages of maturity. Dock is a wonderful shade of green in early May, has a pinkish cast for a short period of two weeks after that, and is a kind of rusty brown on into the fall. Then there are beech, laurel, and spirea leaves to be gathered from our own plantings while the sap is still running briskly. Later the albizzia pods and pine cones must be collected.

All of us at Eighteenth Century Bouquet have summer gardens that produce the more delicate flowers we use in our winter bouquets. The list of plants grown includes many of those known to have been grown by colonial gardeners, but we have neither the time nor the space to meet the demand. Fortunately we have found several retired couples who are happy to help us grow flowers and plant materials for the business.

A few years ago a woman in Pennsylvania began sending us straw-flowers and amaranths from her garden. Now she and her family have an amaranth farm and the barns have been converted into drying sheds. The wife of a former Princeton University dean found many interesting and dryable plants on or near her retirement farm and sent us samples of those she thought we might be able to use in arrangements. Now, collecting these plant materials is her full-time occupation.

But there can be problems in such arrangements. Our favorite grower of tansy, for instance, became suspicious about the quantities we were ordering and eventually refused to sell us any at all. We later learned that she became convinced we were selling tansy for a use to which it had been put by many eighteenth century ladies—for abortions.

As the business has grown, we have all had to specialize more. I now spend a lot of time doing custom arrangements for private homes and historic restorations. Customers often bring favorite containers to the shop and ask that they be filled with flowers that will pick up the colors of a special wallpaper or that will be attractive on a glass and chrome room divider. Requests like these have forced us to be a bit innovative. We have had to learn how to fill aluminum paté molds as well as posy holders and delft bricks, with dried flowers—in the eighteenth century manner.

My current activities also include lecturing on flower arranging in stores that sell our boxes of dried flowers, and speaking at meetings of garden clubs and historic organizations. These talks may not be educational for those who hear them, but I certainly learn a lot as a result of them. The twentieth century members of my audiences frequently send samples of dried plant material we have not known before. Often they write us about their experiments, drying flowers in kitty litter or preserving leaves in anti-freeze, for example.

It was their often repeated questions about the details of arranging that led to the writing of this book. These lovers of flowers were not satisfied with general instructions about arranging—such as using small and light-colored flowers near the top of a bouquet and the larger and darker ones near the rim of the container. It was step-by-step instructions they sought. There were many questions about how far up or out from the container's rim the cockscomb should be, but the most persistent questions had to do with the angles of flower insertions in the various styles of arrangements. So here are the answers of a least one flower arranger.

Often I think back to the phone call that seemed so simple seventeen years ago, and reflect on how different life is now. Then it occurs to me that life isn't so different. The barns are still full of flowers, even though now they are full of drying dock and goldenrod instead of peonies waiting to be taken to market.

2

In the Eighteenth Century Manner

THE ENGLISH LADIES were used to gather great Quantities of Life Everlasting and to pluck them with the Stalks. For they put them with or
without water, amongst other fine Flowers, which they had gathered
both in the Gardens and in the Fields, and placed them as Ornament
in the Rooms.

These are the words of Peter Kalm, a Swedish naturalist and traveler
who visited the New World in the middle of the eighteenth century.
In his *Travels into North America*, we also read that "the Ladies are
much inclined to have fine Flowers all summer long, about or upon the
Chimneys, upon a Table or before a Window, either because of their
Beauty or because of their sweet Scent."

Kalm also gives us some clues as to the practical uses of these arrangements for the eighteenth century householder. Their sweet scent was
not only pleasing in itself, but helped to make the houses more pleasant
in the days when washing machines were nonexistent, bathing was infrequent, and means for neutralizing cooking odors were scarce. During
the winter months when odorless dried flowers decorated the window
sills and sideboards, the ladies strewed about the house those sweet
smelling herbs they had so carefully grown among the flowers. Flowers
were also used to hide the large fireplaces when they were gaping and
empty during the summer. Those who live in present-day houses have
different sets of problems, but it is still true that floral arrangements help
to create a pleasant atmosphere in a room and can enhance almost any
architectural feature.

The colonists are known to have used whatever flowers they could
get, whether these were imported from the Old World, grown in their
gardens and orchards, or gathered in the woods and fields. In their
attempts to make their new homes more familiar, the early settlers
began to import the flowers that they and their forefathers had loved.
These included the blue iris, moss rose, daffodil, veronica, and gilly-

5

flower. During the eighteenth century, the list of imports was greatly expanded to include the peony, more roses, hollyhock, Canterbury bell, larkspur, primrose, pansy, English daisy, and sweet william. Many of the imports did well in the new environment, and a lively market in seeds, bulbs, plants and even seedling trees grew up. Early American newspapers carried advertisements offering tulips, anemonies, poppies, and double larkspur for sale.

Clematis and sumac were among the first native plants to be incorporated into colonial gardens, but these were soon followed by laurel, hydrangea, and phlox. Early American gardeners succeeded in domesticating many of the plants that grew wild in the colonies, but they left some to the woods and fields. Among these was the plentiful goldenrod which they gathered for their household decorations but saw no reason to cultivate.

The flowers of the colonies were so treasured by the gardeners of Europe and especially England that they sent botanists and naturalists to seek out "exoticks" that might be added to their gardens. Through one such endeavor, the approach to Hampton Court was planted in "Golden Rod" which, according to one report, "nods over the whole length of the edge of a walk, three quarters of a mile long, and, perhaps, thirty feet wide, the most magnificent in Europe." Dour New Englanders must have been amazed, for they regarded goldenrod as a plant that would rapidly take over a whole field if one did not check its growth, and scarcely thought of it as a blossom to be cultivated by royalty. Peter Kalm was one among many who visited the colonies for the specific purpose of finding flowers that might be domesticated in their native lands.

The kinds of floral arrangements that were popular in the colonies depended on the geographical area, the affluence of the residents, and the kinds of houses they lived in. Well-to-do settlers in the Old South developed a variety of styles—some large, some small, some of great subtlety and complexity, some that used only a few varieties, and others that were "stuffed" with many. The spacious manor houses of Virginia offered many opportunities for floral displays and the availability of servants and gardeners made it possible to maintain large gardens and to devote many hours to making bouquets for the house.

In New England, where the hewn plank houses were smaller, servants rare, and the climate rigorous, gardens tended to be limited to the utilitarian; floral displays were relatively simple, emphasizing color but composed of fewer different kinds of flowers. The Mid-Atlantic colonies servants and gardeners made it possible to maintain large gardens and to luxuriant as those of the South. Although there are no detailed descriptions of the flower arrangements used in early New England or the Middle colonies, several general accounts do exist. We know quite a lot about the varieties of flowers that were available, the kinds of gardens the people kept, the containers they had to use for arrangements, and the kinds of houses in which the bouquets were displayed.

John Josselyn, an Englishman who visited New England in 1638 and again in 1663, described the dooryard gardens he saw in his book, *New England Rarities*. Other contemporary accounts tell of fenced-in gardens near the houses, where vegetables, utilitarian herbs, and a few flowers that had been transplated from the wild were grown. The walks were wide enough to allow for weeding and havesting, and the beds were of whatever sizes and shapes were convenient and provided the best exposure for the plants. Necessity and expediency were the guides for the garden plans in the early New England and the Mid-Atlantic colonies.

We also know that the fields of New England, New York, New Jersey, and Pennsylvania contained luxuriant stands of black-eyed Susans, asters, and, of course, goldenrod. In the woods and fields there were plentiful supplies of dogwood, laurel, shadbush, and sumac. The first floral arrangements of the rural residents were probably composed of these and other native varieties. Those who lived in the cities, especially the wealthy merchant families of Philadelpha, New York, and Boston, had formal and symmetrical gardens containing a large variety of flowers, including many favorites that had been imported.

In the Brooklyn Botanic Garden's *Handbook on Flower Arrangement*, Margaretta Davis tells us that New England's early floral designs were "simple, casual mixed bouquets using color contrasts rather than harmonious color combinations." The favorite colors, she reports, were red, vermilion, delft blue, lavender, white, yellow, purple, and green. At first, these flowers were probably arranged in pewter mugs and tankards, wooden bowls, and earthenware pots. There were not many places for floral displays in the early houses of rural New England. The simple dwellings of hewn planks were often smaller than the nearby barn. But there was usually a large kitchen, sometimes partitioned off to provide a bed-chamber or a storeroom, a loft above sometimes served as a second bedroom. One can imagine a bowl of wild flowers or a pewter mug containing a few flowers from the dooryard garden on the window sill.

Much more is known about the use of flowers in the southern colonies. Louise Fisher, who for years arranged flowers for the official buildings of Colonial Williamsburg, has described in her *Eighteenth Century Garland* how—by consulting old garden books, the diaries of colonial gardeners, the records of European plant finders, and the correspondence between the avid growers of London and Virginia—she sought to authenticate her arrangements. From this research, she learned much about the gardens and flowers available at the time. But she learned the most from floral prints and portraits that showed bouquets.

In Thomas Sheraton's furniture book, for example, she found illustrations showing "small vases and bowls of flowers and fruits as well as potted plants" on several sideboards. It was, however, Robert Furber to whom she felt most indebted. His 1730 catalog-calendar, *The Flower Garden Display'd*, contained twelve prints of large floral arrangements composed of all the flowers known to bloom in a particular month. These illustrations were in the second edition, offered, "Not only for the Curious in Gardening, but the Prints likewise for Painters, Carvers, Japaners, etc., also for the Ladies, as Patterns for Working, and Painting, in water colours; or Furniture for the Closet." They must also have served as guides for arrangements in eighteenth century Virginia. Mrs. Fisher said she used them more than any other source as guides for the decorations of Colonial Williamsburg.

There is other evidence that Mrs. Fisher's large, "full," "printy," and "buxom" bouquets of many different kinds of flowers and in many colors were popular in the early part of the eighteenth century. Portraits of the period, painted in Virginia and Maryland, show young girls beside tables on which there were just such arrangements. Floral compositions like these, in imported Wedgwood posy holders, bowls of Chinese export china, and Dutch delft bricks, usually come to mind when one thinks of colonial arrangements.

During most of the eighteenth century, Williamsburg was the cultural and horticultural center of the South. Its spacious manor houses were surrounded by well-manicured lawns, raised and geometrically shaped flower beds, shade and fruit-bearing trees. The gardens were filled with favorite flowers imported from England, sweet smelling herbs, and domesticated American varieties. Some of them were formal, in the continental European style; others were more open, reflecting England's recent trend toward a "natural" style. Many of the beds had borders of boxwood and others were enclosed in living walls of shrub roses. Gardens similar to those of Williamsburg's most affluent residents could be found around the homes of many officials and large landholders throughout the South as well as adjoining the residences of wealthy merchants farther north.

The dwellings of the well-to-do offered many settings for floral displays. Most had impressive entry halls where there was ample space for tables bearing bouquets. The bedrooms tended to have plastered walls that were painted in soft blue-greens or gray-blues, providing appropriate backgrounds for smaller and more delicate arrangements. It was in the formal rooms that were likely to be paneled or have the walls covered with painted papers or rich cloth that one found the large floral bouquets in the most opulent imported flower holders.

Less is known about the use of flowers in the simple, clapboard houses of the craftsmen in eighteenth century Williamsburg. But we do know that the gardens of the less wealthy residents were miniatures of the larger and more elegant ones and that they contained most of the same flowers. The expensive imported plants appeared in these gardens considerably later.

Whatever the life style or degree of wealth of eighteenth century Americans, they made good use of the varieties of plants that were available to them, and they adapted floral arrangements to harmonize with the houses in which they lived. The bright colors of the simple bouquet on the New England window sill were as appropriate to that setting as the more subtle shades in the arrangement gracing the dressing table of the governor's wife in Williamsburg. Colonial bouquets were of many types.

Most of the arrangements described in this book are composed in the manner of eighteenth century Williamsburg, but that does not mean they are copies. Some of the materials used today were not available in the 1700's, and many of the techniques for treating flowers were unknown at the time. Suggestions have also been made for arrangements that harmonize with modern styles of architecture, functional furniture, and new building materials, as well as those that go well in older houses with period furniture. The ladies of the Mid-Atlantic colonies whose fresh and dried flowers Peter Kalm so admired, would have done the same. They, too, were using flowers that were unknown to their forefathers and they lived in houses that often differed markedly from those of their Old World relatives. These, the new, then preserve the spirit of the eighteenth century bouquet and capture its flavor so that this colorful decorative art can be enjoyed in our homes today.

3

Preparing Dried Plant Materials: Then and Now

OF ALL THE FLOWERS AVAILABLE for winter bouquets, pearly everlastings and amaranths seem to have been mentioned most in the journals and correspondence of eighteenth century gardeners. From London, there came the reports of Peter Miller that everlastings were "brought to Markets in great Plenty during the Winter Season." He advised that, "when their stalks were put into Glasses with Sand, the Flowers would continue in Beauty till the Spring."

Peter Collinson, whom Mrs. Fisher thought possibly the greatest horticultural correspondent of all time, sent word about the winter use of amaranths. "If the flowers are gather'd in perfection and hung up with their Heads Downwards in a Dry shady Room, they will keep their Colours for years and will make a pleasant Ornament to Adorn the Windows of your parlour or study all the Winter."

The colonists preserved all of their materials for winter bouquets by drying them in the air, either hanging or *in situ*, or by pressing them. Certainly most were hung in bunches with the flower heads down to keep the stems straight; but, when graceful curves were wanted, some flowers and grasses were put in containers of sand immediately after they were picked, and their stems had been stripped of leaves. Those methods are still in use today, as is the colonial technique for pressing leaves, but more recent experiments and materials have expanded the list of potential ingredients for dried bouquets.

Drying Flowers

One of the least expensive and most popular mediums in which to prepare summer's bounty for winter enjoyment is sand. Colonial arrangers used sand to keep flowers in place in their holders, but there is no evidence that they tried to preserve plant materials in it. Indeed the first American description of the technique appeared in December of 1788 in a periodical know as "The American Museum or Repository of Ancient and Modern Fugitive Pieces & Prose and Poetical." But Georgia S. Vance, in her *The Decorative Art of Dried Flower Arrangement*, reports that P. Giovanni Batista Ferrari of Sienna described the sand-drying method in a 1638 book entitled *Flora ouero Cultura de Fiori*. In his chapter on "Dried and Fake Flowers Which Look Fresh and Real," he said the method "was better than the embalming used by the Egyptians" and reported that it had been used in Germany only a few years.

The most modern and certainly the fastest dessicant for removing the moisture from flowers is silica gel. This is the medium used at Eighteenth Century Bouquet, though both sand and borax with cornmeal (the latter an unfortunate experience) have been tried in the past. Once, when some desperately needed bachelor's buttons were drying in cornmeal, we tried to speed up the process in the oven. The resulting blue-studded cornbread was of no help. Since silica gel weighs almost nothing, it is easier than sand on delicate flowers, and considerably easier on the back of the one who has to move the drying containers around. Although gel seems expensive, the cost can be amortized over a long period of time. Its small blue particles disappear to alert the user that it is time to restore the gel's drying properties by baking it. The dessicant can then be used several times before it again needs to be put back in the oven.

Flowers are put down in gel as they are in sand. Excellent instructions are included in the packages of gel, but drawings and descriptions of the positions used are included here for the benefit of those who have the time, space, and stamina to use sand. When more specific instructions for gel drying are necessary, they are included in the Inventory of Dried Plant Materials.

The cardinal rule for drying flowers by any means is that they must be picked at their prime. They must not be fully open or show blemishes of any kind. These are somehow magnified in the drying process.

Silica Gel Drying

Air-tight containers are an absolute necessity for preparing flowers by use of silica gel. The familiar Christmas cake tins are ideal and are plentiful before the holiday season. It is best to stock up in November or early December, because, by the first of the year they are moved to inventory, from which most dealers will not remove them.

It is only efficient to dry flowers with short stems. Too much space and dessicant would be required to prepare them on their long and natural stems. Short-stemmed flowers are easier to work with, particularly in the "stuffed" colonial arrangements. A stem of about one and one-half inches is adequate for all but those flowers that are to be used as the tallest spikes in an arrangement.

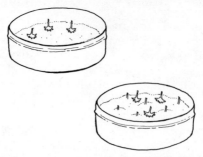

The Face-down Method—All of the composite or daisy-like flowers are dried by this method. Pour about one inch of silica gel into a cake tin and be sure that it is evenly distributed over the bottom of the container. Place the face of a blossom on the gel which you have shaped to "fit" the contour of the flower. Its short stem will then point straight up into the air. Loosely cover the surface of the gel with other flowers, making sure that they do not touch each other. Now, using a small container, such as the cap of an aerosol can, *very gently* shake into the container enough gel to cover the petals and the thick base of the flowers—but not the stems. In the same way, make another layer of blossoms between the stems of those in the first layer and add enough gel to cover those blossoms and come up onto their stems a bit. Finally, seal the lid on the container and store it on a shelf where the container will not be handled and the gel allowed to shift.

The Face-up Method—Many-petaled and three-dimensional flowers— peonies, roses, and some larger marigolds—must be dried in a face-up position. Cover the bottom of a container with about one inch of silica gel and make a hill of the substance that is high enough to accommodate the short stem left on the flower and to support the outside petals. Place in the container as many of the blossoms as it will hold without their either touching each other or the sides of the container. Gently pour more gel *around* the flowers with your right hand as you mound it up next to the outside petals with your left. The outside petals must be quite secure before you begin to sift the gel between the flower petals. If the blossom is very compact, you may need to use a tooth pick to separate the petals as you fill the spaces between them. Finally, fill in between the flowers and the walls of the container until all the flowers are completely covered. Seal and store the container.

The Horizontal Method—Use this method to dry spikes of flowers such as larkspur, small sprays of feverfew-like blossoms, and extra stems that are to be used to lengthen those left on blossoms or to make false stems. Cover the bottom of the drying tin with one inch of gel and lay the flower spikes or sprays on it but not touching each other. Gently sift the silica gel all around the spikes or sprays and then gradually begin to fill in between the individual blossoms. Sometimes you will need to support them with one hand as you sift the gel with the other. On occasion, you will need to separate the blossoms with a tooth pick to allow the gel to fill in around the flower and stem surfaces.

Fern leaves are sometimes dried in gel though they are usually pressed in newspaper. When drying them in gel, lay them out in the pattern you will eventually want on the basic bed of gel. Cover them with about one-half inch of gel, and lay out another two or three layers of leaves. Continue this process until the container is full. Seal the container.

A modified version of this method can be used for small clusters of flowers such as hydrangea and Queen Anne's lace, though both can be dried face down. In these cases, pour one inch of gel into the tin, distribute it evenly, and make a small mound for each flower cluster. Prop the pieces of hydrangea or the head of lace against the mound before you begin to sift the gel between the individual clusters. Be sure all the flowers are adequately covered before sealing and storing the container.

Drying Time—Many arrangers are afraid of using silica because the amount of drying time it takes to preserve blossoms is somewhat unpredictable. The time varies with the amount of moisture in the flowers and in the gel, the relationship between the amount of gel and the number of flowers, and the heaviness of the blossoms and their stems. Single daisies will probably take two or three days; heavy flower spikes can take twelve or fourteen. The important thing to remember is that you will not damage the flowers by opening the tin for a few minutes. Gently move the gel away to see whether they are ready. As in all other aspects of flower arranging, it pays to experiment.

Since flowers dried in gel will reabsorb moisture if exposed in very humid weather, they must be stored carefully. When they have dried adequately but before they become brittle, remove the flowers from the drying container and store them in another air-tight container in which you have put a few tablespoons of gel. Cake tins can be used for storage, but I prefer wide-mouthed Mason jars for smaller blossoms, because they look so pretty and it is somewhat easier to tell what flowers are in what container. Be sure to pack the jars lightly and keep them away from sunlight. A row of jars with dogwood blossoms, bachelor's buttons, and daisies is a joy to behold.

Air Drying

This is by far the simplest method for preparing many flowers and is the only feasible way to handle such large and heavy plant materials as cockscomb, plume celosia, and yarrow. All that is required is a warm, dry, and dark area, but be careful of very hot attics in the summer, for hanging in such places has the effect of the now discredited oven-drying method.

Strip the leaves from the stems of the flowers and make loose bundles by putting a rubber band around the ends of the stems. Do not try to use wire or twist-ems, because the flowers will fall when the moisture has been removed from their stems. Separate the stems in half just below the rubber band and hang the bundle, with the flower heads down, on a clothesline or stretched wire. Smaller flowers, like loosestrife or salvia, can be bundled and hung on coat hangers. One hanger will accommodate five or six small bundles.

As soon as they are thoroughly dry, take the hang-dried materials down and store them in cardboard boxes with tissue paper. Do not try to make the box air tight, for even a little moisture in the plant material will then cause mildew.

Pressing

Leaves and leaf sprays can be preserved by being pressed between sheets of newspaper. Be sure to arrange the leaves to be pressed carefully, because they will come out just as put down. Do not allow one leaf to touch another. Several layers of leaves can be dried as long as there are several sheets of paper between them and a heavy weight is placed on top of the pile.

This method may be used for dogwood, beech, and fern.

Glycerine and Water

Laurel, beech, and magnolia leaves will change in texture and color when allowed to stand in a solution of one part water and two parts of glycerine. The laurel leaves take on a coppery tone; the magnolia leaves become almost leathery as they turn from brown to nearly black, depending on the time they are left in the solution. Beech leaves are a brighter green when they are treated this way than when they are pressed. This is a fascinating process to watch, for you can see the solution moving up to the tips of the leaves.

Pick all leaves while the sap is running vigorously and smash the bottom two inches of the branches. Put the branches in a container filled with three or four inches of the solution as quickly as possible. Do not put them in water first, because they will then absorb less glycerine. When the leaves have turned the color you are looking for or when the solution has reached the tips of the leaves, remove them, dry the wet ends of the branches thoroughly with paper towels, and allow them to air dry for a couple days before storing them in cardboard boxes with tissue paper.

Wiring Flowers

Occasionally dried flowers can be inserted in bouquets on their natural stems, but many must either be wired or given false stems, and most have to be wired for the traditional "buxom" bouquets. African

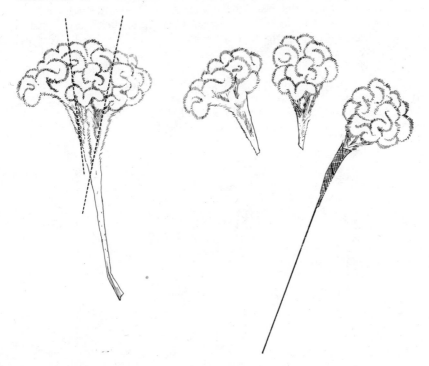

daisies, for example, have such soft stems that they will neither support the blossoms nor go through Oasis, the modern medium for holding the flowers in place. Others, like the magnolia leaves and wood roses, have such thick stems they would crumble the Oasis.

But there are several other compelling reasons for wiring plant materials. It is, for example, too expensive and cumbersome to dry flowers with long stems in silica gel. Drying peonies with their stems would necessitate the use of a huge container and several pounds of gel. Heads of cockscomb are usually much too large and bulky for bouquets; they must be broken into more manageable pieces, each one of which is then wired like a single flower. It is often possible to get three or four "flowers" from one. The same is often true of hydrangea and yarrow, though they do not often make so many flowers. If blossoms are dried with stems that measure one inch or one and one-half inches, however, a minimum amount of space and material is required and none of the wire will show in full arrangements if they are carefully done. Flowers in more open arrangements can be given false stems.

Basic Wiring Techniques

To wire a single flower or a natural spike, lay the end of a length of floral wire along the short stem with which the flower was dried just below the flower or the last flower on the spike. Hold the wire and stem together in your left hand and start wrapping floral tape around them, being sure to pull the tape a bit as you wrap. Eventually you will find that you can twist or twirl the stem and the wire with your left hand as you pull the tape with your right. Tape down below the flower stem and onto the bare wire before tearing off the tape on the roll. If you stop taping at the end of the stem, without firmly attaching some tape to the bare wire, the flower will slip and turn on it.

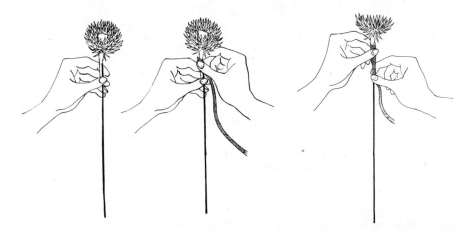

The technique for wiring clusters and spikes is the same, once you have arranged the components properly. The only difference between the two forms is that flowers in a spike are all of different heights. One flower is placed over another always with the smaller flower above the larger ones. The buds of African daisies or peonies, for example, appear above open flowers. Spikes can be made of natural spikes, of single flowers, or of clusters of tiny blossoms. The drawing shows a spike of clusters of immortelle, a spike of natural spikes of blue salvia, and a spike of single amaranth blossoms.

Flowers in clusters are more or less even with one another, or vary only enough to give a slightly rounded effect. Here, too, hold the stems of the flowers alongside the end of a floral wire in your left hand and turn or twirl them as you pull the tape with your right hand. Tape the stems and the wire together from just below the flower heads down below the stems and onto the bare wire. The drawing shows a cluster of pearly everlastings made of small clusters that were broken from a loose and floppy natural cluster.

Occasionally you will find some plant materials that are too heavy for even the heaviest weight of floral wire. This is frequently true of magnolia leaves. If they seem to wobble or twist and turn in the Oasis, you may use two wires, or tape all the way down the wire, or put some glue on the end of the wire before inserting it in the Oasis. In really stubborn cases, all of these devices may be necessary. In any event, when wiring heavy magnolia leaves, allow the wire to go half way up the back of the leaf to provide support for it. Begin taping the stem and the wire together at the base of the leaf and continue taping at least beyond the stem and onto the wire.

With judicious wiring, it is possible to change the shape or form of plant materials. By breaking off the small clusters of white flowers from

the rather loose, open, and often misshapen heads of pearly everlastings, it is possible to make either tighter and neater clusters or attractive spikes of the blossoms. Amaranths, those small, clover-like flowers, would look spotty if used singly in large bouquets, but they are handsome and carry their colors well when two or three are wired together, usually with one over the other to produce a kind of spike.

Natural spikes of blue salvia are invaluable for their color and delicacy, but they would be lost in most arrangements if used individually. When two or three are wired into a rather loose spike, enough of the color is massed to have some impact. Side shoots of goldenrod would also be lost if used singly and the natural sprays are too large and loose for most arrangements. With several shoots wired together as a spike though, their color is concentrated enough to have an effect and they add a lightness and airiness to what might otherwise be heavy and bulky bouquets.

Plant materials that grow in natural sprays are rarely just right for the arrangement you have in mind. German statice grows in a spray composed of several small branches of side shoots on a central and thicker stem. The side branches of shoots are wired in the way you would wire a single flower. Similarly, petticoat lace grows in natural sprays, though it has a somewhat more complicated structure. For more manageable sprays, break off one or two side branches and wire them as you would a cluster or a spike.

When individual flowers like floral buttons are wired into spikes that are to project quite far beyond the base of the bouquet, it is important that the wiring and taping begin low enough so that neither will be visible. If the blossoms in loose spikes are really graduated in height, the amount of visible stem will not be objectionable.

Strawflowers are wired just after they are picked and the blossoms tighten around the wires as they dry. If you buy these flowers, treat the wires that come with them like stems, for the commercially supplied wires are usually too flimsy to hold up in an arrangement. Clip off all but one inch of wire and hold a sturdier wire alongside it. Tape the two wires together and then continue on to the sturdier one. If you grow strawflowers, cut the stem off the blossom and push a wire through the base of the flower and into the center of the blossom, but not so far that it will show. Let them stand upright in a container until the flowers adhere to the wires.

Making False Stems

In open arrangements many flowers, especially those near the top, must be given false stems for wires in these exposed positions would be visible. The use of false stems makes it possible to dry flowers with only short natural stems, thus saving container space and pounds of silica gel. There are three techniques for making such stems.

Frequently the short natural stem can be inserted into the dried stem of another variety of flower. The delicate stem of a delphinium can be lengthened with a pussy willow stem. Make a hole in the willow stem with a pin or a wire, put a drop of glue on the delphinium stem, and simply insert the flower stem in the hole. Queen Anne's lace stems can be used in the same way when a more delicate stem is in order and they are used to lengthen the stems of Queen Anne's lace blossoms that are dried with only short natural stems.

Sometimes the short natural stem of a dried flower cannot be inserted into a false stem. In those cases a piece of wire can be used to connect the flower's stem to the false stem. Cut a short piece of wire and insert half of it into the natural stem and the other half into the false stem. No more than one-half inch of wire need go into each of the stems.

Occasionally flowers need to be made more maneuverable. Elbows of wire permit the manipulation of the direction in which they face. To do this, wire and tape the flower as you ordinarily wire a single blossom. Cut off the wire leaving two inches of wire below the end of the flower's stem. Place the false stem alongside the wire but one inch below the end of the flower stem. Now, retape over the first tape, continue taping over the exposed wire, down and over the wire and the false stem for at least one inch.

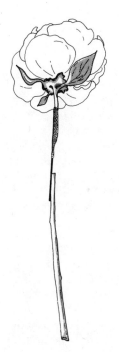

Materials

The only materials needed for wiring plant materials are floral tape, floral wires, Duco cement, and wire clippers. The tape is available in brown and green and the wires in several weights. The ones known as 12 x 18 and 12 x 20 are most useful. The twelve refers to their length and the other number to their gauge, the lower number designating the heavier wire. Arrangers who do not want to bother with the storage of two kinds of wire can use two of the lighter weight ones in place of the heavier one.

4

On Arranging

FEBRUARY IS A CHEERY MONTH for flower arrangers, for it is then that the
seed and plant catalogs appear in the mailbox, bringing promises of a
fragrant spring, a colorful summer, and handsome winter bouquets. Indeed, flower arrangers can look forward to a pleasant schedule of activities throughout the year. When the catalogs arrive, it is time to plan
the year's plantings. In spring those who have gardens set out the plants
and seeds ordered back in February that will produce the materials for
both fresh and dried arrangements. City dwellers find that they can do
surprising things with window boxes and terraces; and both often start
seeds, bulbs, and tubers even before the snow is off the ground.

During spring, summer, and fall there are also wild flowers, pods,
cones, grasses, and leaves to be collected from the fields, along the
roadside, and even in vacant lots. And we have a resource that the
arranger of eighteenth century America did not enjoy. During inclement
weather, we can explore the fresh and dried plant materials in the shops.

Even arrangers who are skilled gardeners will occasionally want some
plant materials that cannot be grown or collected locally. A Northerner
may need magnolia leaves to fan across the back of a traditional arrangement in a posy holder, and an Easterner may want to include some of
the desert's lovely pink petticoat lace in a spring-like bouquet. Large
department stores, garden supply houses, many florists, and some nur-
serymen carry a variety of pods, cones, berries, and dried flowers. Some
supermarkets have impressive amounts of floral buttons, starflowers,
German and domestic statice, and strawflowers during the fall and winter.

All of this growing and collecting—from both the fields and the shops
—is oriented toward the ultimate joy of arranging flowers and greenery
to ornament the environment.

Containers for Colonial Bouquets

The search for containers for colonial arrangements is another en-
joyable occupation of flower arrangers. Probably the most fun is in
finding period pieces at auctions or second-hand shops. Learning to

recognize the authentic ones leads to exciting investigations of glazes and potters' marks used at the time. Occasionally, I suppose, some originals of the more elegant flower holders imported by colonial arrangers may show up, but most of us must be content with today's reproductions. Wedgwood posy holders, delft bricks, and flower horns are available in department stores, gift shops, and the Williamsburg Craft Houses that carry authenticated copies of colonial furniture and household objects. Many of these items can be mail ordered through the catalog of Colonial Williamsburg. Less expensive, and often smaller, versions of the originals, usually made in Japan or Portugal, may be found in gift shops.

But there is evidence that the less affluent colonial arrangers used common household utensils for their flowers. Glass seems not to have been a popular material for flower holders, but it was used, as were containers of earthenware, wood, pewter, and simple porcelain. So today's arranger of colonial bouquets has license to use a variety of flower holders made of many materials. Old but damaged containers can be rescued for dried arrangements, since they need not hold water. Grandmother's cracked sugar bowl can become an authentic and favorite flower holder.

The "Rules" and Techniques

Many insist that there are no rules to follow in arranging flowers. At first, I thought there were few and these had to do with the size of the bouquet relative to the size of the container and the distribution of the flowers by size and shade. I no longer believe that an arrangement must be one and one-half times the height of the container, though it may be a helpful guide to those just starting out. The suggestions for the sorting of blossoms by size and shade remain on the list of rules and techniques as they simplify arranging.

There is a logical and necessary order for placing plant material in these arrangements. The heavier flowers that are to form the base of the bouquet and that block out its basic shape must be inserted first. Often the cockscomb, yarrow, and large strawflowers used for this purpose are almost invisible in the final arrangement. The flowers and other plant materials that are inserted later project out from the container farther and farther until you place the focal points and the tallest spikes.

Probably the single most important concept to keep in mind is that of the gradually changing angle of insertion of flowers. The plant materials at the center-top are perpendicular to the work surface ($90°$). Those inserted around, or at, the rim of the container are horizontal to that surface ($0°$) or are inverted a bit ($-5°$) if breaking the line of the flower holder is the objective. The degree of insertion gets larger and larger as you move from the rim of the container to the top of the arrangement.

Don't start work unless you can afford to take your time. This is especially important for the first work session. It takes time and often

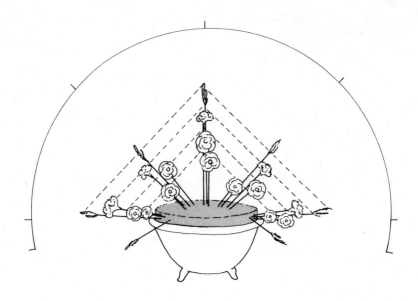

some experimenting to get the feel of the container and to make decisions about which of the available materials will be compatible with it, what size and shape the arrangement should be for its proposed setting, how formal it should be, and how to use the flowers of different colors and weights. Patience may be the most important ingredient.

Before beginning work on any arrangement, prepare your work table. Lay out all the plant materials that may be included along with whatever tools and equipment are likely to be needed.

Wire all of one variety of plant material to be used in the bouquet and stick the wires in a block of Oasis so you can see what you have and determine where each piece is to go. Hold each flower up to the arrangement to see how long the wire should be, then clip the wire and place the flower. Insert all of that variety before starting to wire and place the next.

An arrangement will look spotty and frequently a bit top heavy unless you place the smaller and lighter colored blossoms of each variety near the top of the bouquet and the larger and darker blossoms near the container's rim. Use the medium shades and sizes around or across the middle.

Keep the basic shape in mind as you add all plant materials. The pitfall to be constantly alert for is a bulge in the middle—what we call the pregnant look. The drawing above suggests how flowers are arranged in a bouquet with the basic shape of a cone. The first flowers block out the shape and the flowers added later come out farther and farther, but the outline is retained until the last spikes are added.

Several times during the assembly, get up and walk around the arrangement to see whether there are any holes or thin places in the bouquet. It is important that you get far enough away from the creation to view it as someone would who was walking into the room.

Particular Techniques for Particular Styles

Most colonial bouquets are in one of three forms: all-around bouquets, half-arrangements, or back-to-back arrangements. Particular techniques and procedures are used in each.

All-around Bouquets—These round or conelike arrangements can be viewed from all sides. To distribute the flowers evenly around the bouquet, you must keep turning the container as you insert the plant materials. If you are using a footed bowl that might catch on the work surface, put the bowl on a lazy Susan or a smooth plate so it will turn easily.

Place a flower in the center of the Oasis and then horizontally insert some of the same kind of blossoms in an irregular row at the rim of the container. A few of these may go a bit above the rim, and a few may be inverted enough to break the container's rim. Next, make an irregular row around the middle—or zig-zag the blossoms around it. In many of these bouquets there is another row around, but just below, the center flower and in large arrangements there is more than one zigzagged row around the middle.

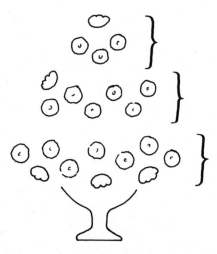

Repeat essentially this pattern with other varieties of flowers, gradually bringing them farther out from the container. Often you will feel that you are inserting many blossoms in the same place, but that is what produces the buxom look so characteristic of colonial bouquets.

Half-arrangements—These arrangements are meant to be placed against a wall or on a mantle where they will be viewed from only three sides. Most are begun with a background in the shape of a fan. The more formal creations of the colonial South often had fans of magnolia leaves, but fans can be made of many plant materials—laurel or dogwood leaves, fertile or sterile fern, or any of many kinds of spikey materials.

Essentially a half-arrangement is made of a series of fans of leaves and flowers and a central mass of larger and darker blossoms and a few spikes. In the Franklin urn arrangement, for example, there are fans of magnolia leaves, goldenrod, African daisies, immortelle, tansy, amaranth, domestic statice, large and small floral buttons, larkspur, and black grass. Naturally the fans made later are smaller than the early ones, since subsequent additions are either inserted in an established fan or in front of one. The effect of these fans is to create a movement toward the central mass.

The central mass is made of larger and more sturdy plant materials, some of which are inserted in a rather stylized pattern. The arrangement in the Franklin urn has crossed diagonal lines of yellow and orange marigolds for its focal points.

Turn the container of a half-arrangement frequently as you work to check its profile. Here, too, you must make sure that a bulge does not develop in its middle. Even though the plant materials that are added to the central mass come out farther and farther, the basic profile of a right-angled triangle must be maintained. That also means that the back must be flat.

To make a back fan for a half-arrangement, start with the largest leaf and place it in the center back of the Oasis, no more than one-quarter inch from the very back edge. Then, using pairs of smaller and smaller leaves, place one to the left and one to the right of the center leaf, and then one to the left and one to the right of the already placed leaves until you get close to the ends of the Oasis. The smaller leaves near the ends start to come forward in the Oasis, and the last one on each side hangs over the front corner of the container.

If a half-arrangement is to be placed in front of a mirror or anyplace where the back will be even partially exposed, it must be finished. Cut off any wires that have come through the Oasis and are sticking out the back. Then, with the back facing you, make a series of smaller and smaller leaf fans with the glossy surface of the leaves facing you. Be sure that none of the leaf tips are visible from the front of the arrangement and that there are enough fans to cover the Oasis and all wires. If you do not have enough small leaves for the lower fans, simply trim some of the larger ones with ordinary scissors. The back of a half arrangement can be finished with fans of statice or goldenrod instead of leaves.

Back-to-Back arrangements—These bouquets are oblong, either rectangles or ovals, that can be viewed from any direction. Begin these arrangements by making a fan along the center of the Oasis, going from one end to the other and jutting out over the rim of the container at those ends. The order for placing plant materials in these fans is the same as for placing those at the back of a half arrangement, except that on occasion you place a flower in the center of the Oasis, then place those that are to go over the ends of the container, and proceed by placing flowers to the left and right of first the center flower and then to the left and to the right of those.

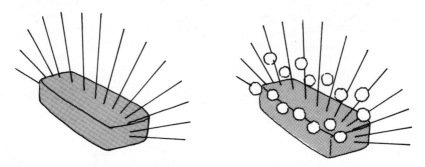

Except for inserting the materials used in the fan, place all of one variety of flower on one side of the arrangement, turn the container, and repeat the pattern on the other. Flowers are placed in two or three irregular rows—one at the rim of the container, one across the middle of the arrangement, one below the fan. Check the narrow ends of the bouquet before introducing a new kind of plant material to make sure that they are not being neglected and becoming thin.

Tools and Equipment for Arrangers

It is much easier to work at a well prepared table, for it is distracting to have to get up and look for equipment. You will need wire clippers to adjust the length of flower "stems," scissors to trim leaves, tweezers to use in inserting at least the last flowers in very full bouquets, and a knife to shape Oasis for the flower holder or liner. A ruler is also useful, especially in following the instructions for the arrangements described here.

The equipment needed for different arrangements varies, but a well equipped work table will include the floral wires described earlier and the materials listed below.

Oasis is useful for holding flowers between the time they are wired and the time they are put into the arrangement. At least one more block of Oasis will be necessary for preparing the container. Be quite sure that you ask for it by its trade name and that you are not given styrofoam by mistake. Styrofoam is stiff and much less easy to work with.

Papier mache liners are excellent for protecting delicate flower holders that might be damaged if Oasis were glued to them. They are lightweight, available in many sizes and shapes, and can be purchased from most florist shops and garden supply houses. Frequently though you will find that cereal bowls, cups, cans, and the tops of large aerosol cans will work just as well. The liner must be put in the permanent container before you begin work on the arrangement.

Floral clay, which is sold in the shape of a long coil, is useful for anchoring liners to flower containers.

When you do not feel it is necessary to use a liner, you can glue the Oasis directly into the container. Be sure that you use a water soluble glue that can be removed by simply soaking the container after you have dismantled the arrangement.

Duco cement is the adhesive I like to use on fragile flowers. African daisy blossoms, for example, will often fall off their stems unless they are secured. Run a little of the cement down the short stem and onto the base of the flower. Fallen petals of rudbeckia blossoms can also be put back in place with Duco.

Floral tape, which is used to secure short flower stems to floral wires, is available in brown and green. I usually use the brown one, but choose whichever you think will be the least obtrusive or look more like the natural stem of the particular blossom.

Adhesive tape can be used to secure Oasis to a flower holder if you want to begin work before the glue is completely dry. Criss-cross the tape from one edge of the container, across the Oasis, and onto the opposite edge. Clip off the visible ends of the tape after you have finished the bouquet.

Floral picks are long and thin pieces of green wood with one pointed end and a wire attached to the other. These are sometimes used as substitute flower stems, but, when the wire is removed, they are especially useful in securing one layer of Oasis to another.

Florist sprays are available in many colors and there is a clear one. Floral buttons and salvia spikes can be sprayed to match a particular shade in wallpaper or rugs. The clear one can be used to add a sheen to berries and leaves.

Preparing Flower Holders

In most instances the flower holder can be prepared for an arrangement by simply cutting a piece of Oasis to fit the container's opening and pushing the Oasis in just far enough to leave one inch or one and one-half inches of the material projecting above the rim of the flower holder. Always make an impression of the opening by inverting the container on the top of the Oasis and then cut through the three-inch-thick block. That way you will be cutting with its grain and the material will crumble less as you insert the flower wires.

Remember that you do not have to completely fill the container with Oasis. If you are using a tall and narrow container, you may find that it will have to be weighted. In that case, simply pour a little sand into the bottom of the flower holder, and then push Oasis into its mouth.

Traditional Arrangements

Mantles, window sills, and fireplaces were about the only places the early colonists had for displaying floral decorations. Their "dining" tables of plain wood were set in the middle of the kitchen, the main living space in those early homes, and there were no chests or desks or small tables for bouquets. That is no doubt why so many of their arrangements were what we call half-arrangements, those that could be viewed from only three sides and were placed in front of a backdrop. Many of these had fans across the back of the other plant materials. In the South, where magnolia trees grow so luxuriantly, these readily available leaves were used for the fans. It is half-arrangements with magnolia fans that most of us think of as the traditional decorations of the eighteenth century, although many other styles also became popular.

As life became less rigorous and living space was expanded, there were separate rooms for dining, and centerpieces began to appear, but they were edible. Bowls or épergnes held attractive arrangements of the country's plentiful fruits and nuts within easy reach of all the diners. Eventually more incidental furniture was introduced and these additional pieces provided space for bouquets in various sizes and shapes.

Six of the eight arrangements included in this group of traditional compositions are half-arrangements. Two can be viewed from all sides, but even these use the concept of the central fan. We call these back-to-back bouquets and they are, in fact, much like two connected half-arrangements. The posy holder and the Franklin urn contain traditional fans of magnolia leaves and stylized lines across the central mass. Laurel leaves make a fan for the tea caddy and spikey flowers and ferns are fanned at the back of the other half-arrangements. The central fans for the bouquets in the delft brick and the cachepot are also made of flowers.

All of these traditional arrangements are composed of a number of different kinds of plant materials and include a wide variety of contrasting colors. The arrangement in the posy holder, for example, is made of fifteen varieties of flowers and leaves in ten colors: the one in the Franklin urn contains sixteen plant materials in seven distinct colors.

Ingredients used in the arrangements are listed in the order in which they are inserted.

A Yellow and Blue Bouquet in a Delft Brick

See color pages for illustration.

Holland delft bricks in blue and white were among Queen Mary's favorite flower containers and rapidly gained popularity in northern Europe and the American colonies. The top of each has a pattern of large and small holes that were designed to help the arranger keep her flowers in place though they were sometimes used to hold ink and quills on eighteenth century writing tables. This solid and somewhat formal arrangement of yellows and blues is easily carried by the brick, and the blues of the salvia and domestic statice pleasantly pick up the color of its cobalt blue decorations. Black-eyed Susans, a favorite colonial flower, are the focal points of the bouquet.

The finished arrangement is fourteen inches high and fifteen inches long. It is low enough for a dining table, but would also be attractive on a desk, a room divider, or a book case.

Cinquefoil—Seventy clusters of leaves and unopened buds, wired into twenty-seven spikes of two or three.

Yellow yarrow—Twenty-two pieces, either small heads or one and one-half inch clusters made of pieces broken from larger heads, wired.

White African everlastings—Twenty-eight to thirty buds and flowers, most flowers wired singly, but smaller flowers wired into spikes with buds above them to make a total of twenty-two pieces.

Large white strawflowers—Fourteen flowers, wired singly.

Miniature yellow strawflowers—Four wired singly and twenty-eight wired in fourteen spikes of two blossoms, the smaller above the larger.

Yellow immortelle—Small clusters of blossoms broken from large heads and wired into twenty-eight spikes of eight to ten blossoms.

Blue statice—Twenty-eight natural clusters, two to three inches long or smaller pieces wired to that length.

Black-eyed Susans—Twenty flowers, wired singly.

Blue salvia—Sixty-nine natural spikes, wired into twenty-three spikes of three.

White miniature floral buttons—Twenty-nine loose spikes of fourteen to fifteen individual buttons, wired.

Preparing the Container

The delft brick is three and three-quarter inches high, six and one-half inches long, and two and one-quarter inches thick. Pour sand into the holes on the top of the brick until it comes to within one and one-half inches of its top. Cut a piece of Oasis into tiny pieces and push them tightly on top of the sand in the brick. It will crumble as you distribute it across the top and pack it firmly. Cut from a block of Oasis, a piece that measures five and one-half inches by two inches by two inches. Place that piece of Oasis on top of the brick and secure it in position by inserting floral picks into the Oasis, through the holes in the top of the brick, and into the crumbled Oasis below. Put one pick in the large center hole and two through small holes on either side of the large one.

The Assembly

This is to be an oval arrangement that can be viewed from any direction, so you must follow the rules that apply to back-to-back arrangements. With one of the broad sides of the brick facing you, place one variety of plant material, then turn the container and repeat the pattern with the same kind of flower. Be sure to inspect the ends before beginning work with the next plant material. They must not be too thin, and they will not be if you work back far enough on either side of the arrangement. But check on this frequently.

Use the spikes of moss green cinquefoil to sketch the outline of the bouquet. Place a spike in the middle of the Oasis with its tip eleven and one-half inches from the table. With one of the broad sides facing you, insert a spike just over the rim of the brick at either corner and place two between them. Next insert one at each end. All of these project about two inches beyond the brick's rim. Now, with seven spikes, make two irregular rows between the tall center spike and those at the rim. The lower row is made of four spikes and the one above it with three. Turn the brick around and repeat the pattern for all but the center spike on the other side.

Clusters of yellow yarrow are used to make the base of the arrangement. Very little of it will show in the final bouquet. When placing the yarrow, be sure to push the clusters in farther than the cinquefoil spikes which should come out one inch or one and one-half inches farther than the yellow clusters. Using eleven pieces for each side, insert them in the spaces between the cinquefoil spikes.

Use eleven of the all-white African everlastings for each side. Place one below and on either side of the top spike of cinquefoil. Make an irregular row of five above the rim of the brick and another of four about halfway up the arrangement. All of these are brought farther out than the clumps of yarrow, but not so far as the spikes of cinquefoil.

The large white strawflowers come out about as far as the African everlastings and are placed in three rows among them. Place one between the African everlastings near the top of the arrangement and make two irregular rows of three flowers, one above the rim of the brick and one about halfway up the arrangement.

The miniature yellow strawflowers come out about one and one-half inches farther than the large strawflowers. Two of the single flowers go near the strawflowers at the top of the arrangement. Place four of the doubles just above the strawflowers at the rim of the brick and three doubles in an irregular row halfway between those at the top and those above the rim. Repeat on the other side.

Now start to bring the spikey flowers out from the white strawflowers and African daisies. When making rows of these be sure to work back far enough on either side so that some of every kind of flower is in that fan that runs from one end of the brick, to the other.

The spikes of yellow immortelle blossoms also come out about one and one-half inches farther than the large strawflowers. Place one spike just off center at the top of the arrangement and one a little lower and on either side of that one. Make an irregular row of six over the rim of the container and zig-zag five across the broad middle of the bouquet. Repeat the pattern on the other side.

The spikes of blue statice come out one and one-half inches farther than the white strawflowers and African everlastings. Place one just off center at the top of the arrangement. Make an irregular row of six spikes above the rim of the brick and one of three below the single spike at the top. Zig-zag four spikes across the broad middle of the arrangement. Repeat on the other side and inspect the ends.

The black-eyed Susans are the focal points of the bouquet so they must come out farther than the large strawflowers and African everlastings, but be careful that their wires do not show. Place two blossoms just below the immortelle at the top of the arrangement. Make two irregular rows, each of four flowers, one row above the rim of the brick and one across the middle of the arrangement. Repeat the pattern on the other side.

The highest point in the arrangement is a spike of blue salvia whose tip is fourteen inches from the table top. Put one spike a little below and on either side of it. Make an irregular row of five spikes above the rim of the brick and zig-zag four across the middle of the arrangement. All of these come out two and one-half to three inches farther than the large strawflowers and African everlastings. Repeat the rows.

The spikes of white miniature floral buttons come out as far as possible without the tape showing. For the most part, this means they will come out about as far as the spikes of blue salvia. Place one spike at top center, but lower than the tallest spike of blue salvia. Place one to the left and one to the right of that. Then, starting at the rim of the container and working up, make irregular rows of five, four, and three spikes. Turn the container and repeat.

Possible Substitutions

If you are unable to get some of the plant materials called for in this arrangement, here are some suggested substitutions. For the yarrow, you might use blonde cockscomb. Goldenrod could substitute for the blue salvia, and yellow strawflowers might take the place of the white ones and the African everlastings. The silvery artemisia 'Silver King' could replace the white miniature floral buttons. Either marigolds or yellow zinnias might be used instead of the black-eyed Susans and orangy amaranths could stand in for the miniature yellow strawflowers.

A Tea Caddy of Pods and Laurel Leaves

Many textures of plant materials in woodsy and earthy colors bring out the grain and the sheen of this handsome mahogany container. A Chippendale tea caddy is sturdy enough to carry a collection of heavy and dramatic pods, leaves, and flowers that would overpower most containers. The total effect is not delicate, but it is beautiful. The focal points of the arrangement are both of the eighteenth century—the yellow yarrow, a favorite at Williamsburg, and the pods of the cotton plant, introduced in the South by Philip Miller, one of the best known botanists of that era. There is a marvelously bright and lustrous surface on the inside of the cotton pods, and the banana-like okra pods are powerful additions.

Because of the heaviness of the caddy and the plant materials, a large and informal setting seems required. A library, den, or a paneled room would be ideal. The arrangement is twenty inches wide, fifteen inches high, and eleven inches deep.

Laurel leaves—Seventeen three-to-five-leaf sprays of glycerine-treated leaves taken from the tips of the branches, wired when necessary for height..

Rusty cockscomb—Eight pieces, one and one-half inches in diameter, either small heads or pieces broken from large heads, both wired.

Yellow yarrow—Six pieces, two and one-half inches in diameter, either whole heads or pieces broken from larger heads, the latter wired.

Okra pods—Eight pods, wired.

Cotton pods—Eleven pods, five wired singly and six wired in three spikes of two.

Pine cones—Twenty-five small cones, wired into nine spikes of two or three.

Golden plume celosia—Seven spikes made either of the delicate tips after the side shoots have been removed or of several side shoots, both wired.

Pink dock—Twelve side shoots, wired in six spikes of two.

Orange amaranths—Twenty-five blossoms, wired into ten spikes of two or three.

Preparing the Container

It is not difficult to convert a tea caddy into a container for dried flowers without destroying it for future use—for tea, for jewelry, or just for decoration. First remove the foil-lined dividers that once separated the varieties of tea in the ten inch long and four inch high box. Cut from a block of Oasis a piece that is six inches long and four inches wide and push it into a papier mache liner of that size. On top of that, add another piece of Oasis one and one-half inches high, to raise the height to four and one-half inches. Secure the second piece to the first by inserting floral picks through both pieces at the center and the back. Trim off the exposed ends of the picks.

To avoid a pregnant look in the finished arrangement, trim one and one-half inches off the front of the top layer of Oasis. Anchor the filled liner to the bottom of the tea caddy with floral clay. Finally, to be sure the lid does not fall forward and damage the arrangement, twist the middle of a rather heavy wire around the lock on the lid and insert the ends of the wire deeply in the Oasis at the front corners of the liner.

The Assembly

The shape of the arrangement is established with sprays of laurel leaves. They do not have to be wired unless additional height is required or the natural stems are so thick that they will either crumble the Oasis or take up so much space that there will not be room for stems to be added later. Starting at the center back of the Oasis, insert a spray of leaves whose tip is thirteen inches from the table. With six more sprays of leaves and working first to the left and then to the right of the already placed leaves, make a fan with the last spray on either side inserted horizontally just above the rim at the back of the box. Horizontally insert a leaf spray just over the rim at front center but do not allow the leaves to obscure the lock. Put a spray at each of the front corners, allowing them to hang over the box. Finish that row by placing a spray between the center one and those at each corner. These should be inserted in a more upright position so the row at the rim is irregular. Using five more sprays, construct a fan between the back fan and the row at the rim.

Rusty cockscomb makes the base of the arrangement. Place the clusters between the laurel leaves but do not let them project out and up as far as the leaves. Use three pieces in a top row at the back of the box, two at its front rim, and three in a middle row.

Next, place two of the largest pieces of yellow yarrow above the rim of the box. The largest should go above the lock, but not hide it and the other a little lower and to its right. Insert a piece at either end so it faces out over the end. Now place a piece of yarrow above and to the left of the one over the lock and another above and to its right. The yarrow heads project out and up as far as the cockscomb. Here again you may use the natural stems, since they need not be flexible and you can this way avoid having to hide too many wires.

If possible, select okra pods with graceful curves. Place four in both the back and the middle rows. Allow the pods to project well out beyond the leaves in the middle row and to rise above those in the back row by one or two inches.

Place one of the spikes of cotton pods above the cockscomb to the right of the lock and the other two near the center of the arrangement. Put a single cotton pod over each of the front corners of the box and insert the others around the spikes of pods near the arrangement's center.

Push the pine cones in farther than or below the leaves and the cotton and okra pods. Use six in the back fan, but not quite in its center. Place one over the rim of the caddy, just to the left of the lock. Put one on either side of the center piece of yarrow.

Use five spikes of plume celosia to make a fan in front of and below the fan of laurel leaves at the back of the arrangement. Place a spike on either side of the exact center of the arrangement.

Insert the spikes of pink dock in vague or fanlike patterns across the back and middle of the arrangement, especially where you can see holes.

Finally add the spikes of orange amaranths. Fan four of the smaller spikes across the back and place one above the rim of the container on either side of its center. Insert four across the middle of the arrangement. These come up and out about as far as the pine cones.

Possible Substitutes

If you want to lighten this bouquet for a dark corner, you might use lagurus, wheat, or goldenrod in place of the plume celosia. Wheat or a tan reed would be lighter than the dock, and white amaranths might take the place of the orange ones.

A Traditional Bouquet in a Franklin Urn

A Franklin urn is a replica of the water container found on top of the old, cast-iron, wood-burning stoves. This precursor of modern humidifiers is black with a greenish or bluish cast, suggesting the corrosion of iron by water.

The mostly yellow and gold arrangement has the typical eighteenth century feeling because it is stuffed with so many different kinds of plant materials. That feeling is intensified by the fan of magnolia leaves so popular with southern flower arrangers of the period. A room with colonial decor would be an ideal setting for this bouquet, but it would also be attractive in an office, a den, a library, or in any large room with not too delicate furniture. The weight and color of the container and the leaves, as well as the massing of flowers, make a French provincial room inappropriate. The half-arrangement needs a backdrop of some kind. It would be superb on a mantle, in the center or off to one side and balanced by a pair of candleholders. It is eighteen inches high and nineteen inches wide.

Brown magnolia leaves—Thirteen glycerine-treated leaves, wired and taped to the bottom of the wire.

Golden cockscomb—Five pieces, one and one-half to two inches in diameter, either small heads or pieces broken from larger heads, wired.

Orange marigolds—Three blossoms, two inches in diameter, wired singly.

Yellow marigolds—Two blossoms two inches in diameter, wired singly.

Large white (cream) strawflowers—Five flowers, one and one-half inches in diameter, wired singly.

Goldenrod—Fifteen to twenty natural sprays, thirteen wired as they are, the rest broken into individual side shoots and wired into spikes of two or three shoots each.

White African daisies—Twenty-seven blossoms, five of the larger ones wired singly and twenty-two wired into eleven spikes of two each, with a smaller flower above a larger one.

Yellow immortelle—Eighty individual blossoms, wired into eleven spikes of seven or eight blossoms.

Yellow yarrow—Five pieces, one to one and one-half inches in diameter, either small whole heads or pieces broken from large heads, wired.

Yellow tansy—Twenty-five to thirty button-like clusters, wired into twelve spikes of two or three clusters.

White (cream) amaranths—Eighteen blossoms, wired into six
  spikes of three blossoms each.
White domestic statice—Eleven to eighteen long pieces of statice,
  wired into eleven spikes that are two inches long.
Orange or rust miniature strawflowers—Fourteen to twenty-one
  flowers, wired into six one-inch clusters of two or three
  blossoms.
Large white floral buttons—Thirty-five buttons, wired into seven
  spikes of five each.
Miniature white floral buttons—One hundred and fifty individual
  buttons, wired into nine loose spikes of fifteen to eighteen each.
White larkspur—Seven tips of natural larkspur spikes, measuring
  four inches, wired.
Lagurus—Fourteen to eighteen grass heads, wired into seven spikes
  of two each, unless they are very small.
Golden plume celosia—Ten spikes made of side shoots broken from
  the large plumes, wired.
Black grass—Five natural spikes on their own stems.

Preparing the Container

The urn is seven inches long, four inches wide, and five and one-half
inches high, but the opening is smaller. For it, cut a piece of Oasis
five and one-half inches long and three and one-half inches wide. It
must be high enough to extend one and one-half inches above the rim
of the urn. Secure the Oasis to the container with water-soluble glue
so it will not damage the container. If you want to begin work on the
arrangement before the glue has had a chance to dry thoroughly, criss-
cross adhesive tape from the edge of the urn over the Oasis to the
opposite edge. The ends of the tape can be snipped off later.

The Assembly

Already prepared magnolia leaves can be purchased from dried flower
suppliers. If you are going to prepare your own, cut off all but one-half
inch of the natural stems which are usually thick and brittle and often
crooked. Lay a long wire along the short stem so that one end goes
about half way up the back of the leaf and the other extends down well
beyond the end of the leaf's natural stem. Start taping the natural stem
and the wire together at the base of the leaf and continue taping down
to the end of the wire. If, when you start to arrange them, you find
you have trouble keeping the heavy leaves in place, put a drop of Duco

cement on the end of the wire just before inserting it in the Oasis. You may use two wires if you think you need an even sturdier stem. Be sure all the wires are deeply inserted in the Oasis.

Begin the arrangement by fanning seven magnolia leaves across the back of the Oasis. The wires should be inserted no more than one-quarter inch in from the back edge of the Oasis. The tip of the center leaf will be seventeen inches from the top of the table. Working from that leaf and using pairs of leaves that are smaller and smaller and have shorter and shorter stems, put a leaf to the left and then one to the right of the already placed leaves. These leaf tips are sixteen, thirteen, and nine inches from the top of the table. Now begin to come forward along the outside edge of the Oasis, putting two leaves at either end of the urn and allowing them to extend over the side by first five and then four and one-half inches. Finally, put a leaf at each of the front corners of the urn, making sure that the one on the right is bent down over the rim of the container more than the one on the left.

With three pieces of cockscomb, establish a diagonal line from the upper left of the fan to the lower right. One piece is two inches below the second from the center leaf, one is seven inches below the center leaf, and the other is two inches above the last leaf on the lower right. Insert the fourth piece three inches above the lower left leaf, and the last one three inches below the second from the center leaf on the right. All of these must be bent so the heads of cockscomb are facing out, not up as they would naturally do.

The crossed lines established by the cockscomb are the keys to the placement of all of the rest of the plant material to be used in the central mass of the arrangement. Notice that the line from the top left to the bottom right is considerably longer than the one crossing it. It is the difference between the lengths of these lines that insures that the final arrangement will not look box-like. The top pieces of cockscomb are inserted toward the back of the Oasis, the center one is slightly forward, and the lower ones are in front of that. Most of the flowers will be in front of the cockscomb so it must not come too far forward.

The marigolds are to be the focal points of the arrangement. Starting just below the cockscomb on the upper left, insert the three orange marigolds between and out as far as the pieces of cockscomb in that line, with the third marigold just below the piece of cockscomb at the lower right. Remember that the larger flowers always go at the bottom of an arrangement and the smaller ones at the top. Now insert the yellow marigolds between the pieces of cockscomb in the crossing line. Notice that the stronger color, the orange, was used for the dominant line that moves from the upper left to the lower right.

Insert five large white, really cream, strawflowers between the marigolds and the cockscomb of the crossed diagonals.

Make a fan of the thirteen whole sprays of goldenrod just in front of the fan of leaves, keeping the tips of the sprays two inches below the tips of the leaves. Be sure to start with the center of the fan, and then place the sprays in pairs. First place one on the left and then one on the right of those already in position. Be sure to place goldenrod in front of the leaves at the front corners of the container. Now, to enhance the circular movement created by the fan of leaves and the strong diagonal line from upper left to lower right, select some side shoots or tips of goldenrod that naturally curve to the right and wire them into spikes of two or three shoots. Insert these in the fan of goldenrod sprays. All of them must curve to the right even though half of them are to the left of the center of the arrangement. Insert four more spikes of side shoots among the cockscomb and marigolds, but allow them to project out two or two and one-half inches beyond the flower heads. These begin the softening of the arrangement and avoid a flat look.

Make a fan of the eleven spikes of white African daisies in front of and a little lower than the goldenrod fan. Horizontally insert one of the largest single flowers in the center front, just above the rim of the urn. This will help to hide the Oasis. Use the remaining daisies to fill in holes in the central mass of the arrangement.

Use seven spikes of yellow immortelle to create still another fan in front of the goldenrod fan, but do not allow it to project up and out so far. Fill in holes in the central mass with the other four spikes, allowing them to come out only about one-half inch farther than the cockscomb. Because the immortelle spikes are not so light and feathery as those made of goldenrod, they must not come out so far.

With the yellow yarrow, return to the diagonal lines established with the cockscomb and marigolds. Again, starting at the upper left and moving to the lower right, place three pieces between the marigolds and the pieces of cockscomb. Then place one in the lower left and one in the upper right of the crossing diagonal.

Insert seven of the spikes of yellow tansy in front of and a little below the fan of immortelle spikes. Place the other five spikes in the central mass so they jut out beyond the cockscomb by only about one and one-half inches.

Stop now and take a look at what you have done so far. Fill in what holes you see with side shoots of goldenrod that have been wired as spikes.

Again, go back to the fan. By now you will need fewer flowers to make a fan, because you will have moved toward the center of the arrangement with the addition of each new plant material introduced. Five spikes of white amaranths will be enough and they should come out about one and one-half inches farther than the cockscomb. Continue work on the fan by starting in the middle and then placing material to the left, then the right of the already placed material. The sixth spike goes in the middle of the central mass.

It still seems as though the arrangement needs more fill, but goldenrod would tend to darken it. Use white domestic statice to add lightness and brightness. Insert seven spikes in front of the original goldenrod fan, but do not let them come up and out so far. Insert three or four more spikes in the central mass and allow them to come out two inches farther than the cockscomb.

Return to the diagonal lines to place the rusty miniature strawflowers. Use five clumps in those lines as you have used other flowers there. Put the sixth one next to the white African daisy in the center front, just over the rim of the container.

By now all of the holes should have been filled and the flatness of the central mass has been broken by the spikes of white statice and amaranths, but the bouquet would benefit from a still lighter and more airy look. For this use spikes of both large and miniature floral buttons. When wiring these, retain as much of the natural stems as possible, for they are to project up and out five inches farther than the cockscomb and none of the taping or wire must be allowed to show. Use five spikes of the large buttons beside the immortelle in the fan and projecting beyond it. Place two in the central mass. Intersperse five spikes of the miniature buttons among those of the large ones and insert four in the central mass. As you continue inserting material in the back fan, you may find that the leaves tend to bend backward. If they do, just push them forward again, or you will find that you are forever filling in that space. In the end, when you finish off the back, everything will be appropriately pushed forward.

Remember to turn the urn frequently so you can check the profile of the arrangement.

Still another spike and some more white seem in order. White larkspur is the solution to that problem. Use the tips of the natural spikes. If there are a lot of tiny buds on the tip, and some space between them and the actual flowers, cut off the tiny buds and the empty stem, but be sure that you do not have an awkward blunt end. Insert five of these spikes beside the immortelle in the fan and place two in the central mass, one above the center piece of cockscomb and one an inch or two below it. These are to project out five inches farther than the cockscomb.

Make a fan of five spikes of fuzzy lagurus about four inches from the center of the arrangement. They should come out about as far as the larkspur. Use two lagurus spikes in the central mass.

With seven spikes of golden plume celosia, make another fan in front of but a little below the goldenrod fan. Intersperse three spikes in the central mass, about five inches from its absolute center.

Since both the container and the leaves are dark, it is a good idea to move just a touch of that darkness toward the center of the arrangement. Use black grass for this purpose. Five grass heads will be enough. Insert them in the inner part of the fan, next to the immortelle.

If the arrangement is going to be placed against a wall or anyplace that will hide its back, all you have to do to finish it is to make two hairpinlike structures of heavy wire and insert them in the back of the Oasis so they push the magnolia leaves forward. If the urn is to go in front of a mirror, however, the back must be made more presentable. For that, follow the instructions on page 27.

A Cachepot of Pinks

See color pages for illustration.

According to Webster, a cachepot is a cover for a flower pot, but many use the word to mean a catch-all or hiding place. The cachepot, filled with pink flowers and berries, is a small oval pot with an ornate cover, a replica of a water urn found on top of a cast iron, wood-burning stove. Its color is smoky blue, sometimes called verdi green, that suggests the corrosion of iron by water. Eighteenth century ladies also used containers like this for storing rose petals and sweet-smelling herbs to perfume their rooms.

This mostly pink arrangement has accents of apple green in the hydrangea in various stages of maturity and of darker green in the maidenhair fern. All of the other plant materials in this fresh and summery bouquet are in shades of pink.

The rather informal arrangement is fourteen inches high, nineteen inches wide, and eleven inches thick at the middle of the container's rim. The bouquet would be handsome on a mantle, in a corner cupboard, on a desk, or on almost any table that is not round but is large enough to carry the mass of color. It is not, however, meant for a rustic setting.

The same design might be used for a yellow arrangement or a blue and white one, both on a base of blonde cockscomb and using maidenhair fern. For the yellow bouquet, substitute yellow strawflowers, African daisies, snapdragons, and off-white amaranths. Yellow statice could take the place of the berries, but no substitute would be necessary for the green hydrangea. The blue and white arrangement could be made of white strawflowers, amaranths, African daisies, larkspur, and snapdragons with blue hydrangea and statice.

Pink cockscomb—Nineteen small heads or one and one-half inch pieces broken from larger heads, wired.

Large-flowered green hydrangea—Seventeen to nineteen one and one-half to two-inch pieces of large flowered hydrangea, broken from large heads, wired, coated with clear floral spray.

Large pink strawflowers—Thirteen, wired singly.

Pink African daisies—Forty-two daisies wired into twenty-one spikes of two with the smaller flower above the larger.

Pink pepper berries—Twenty-three three-inch spikes made of small clusters broken from large sprays, wired, coated with clear floral spray.

Pink amaranths—Thirty-eight blossoms, wired into nineteen spikes of two.

Small-flowered green hydrangea—Twelve one and one-half to two-inch pieces, broken from large heads, wired, coated with clear floral spray.

Pink snapdragons—Fifteen natural spikes with buds at the top, five
   to six inches long, wired.
Maidenhair fern—Seventeen natural sprays measuring up to three
   inches long, wired.

Preparing the Container

The shape of the cachepot makes it a particular favorite of flower
arrangers. Most pedestal containers are round and too high for very
versatile arrangements. The cachepot is three and one-half inches high,
six inches long, and three inches deep in the middle.

Because you are not likely to find either a papier-mache or glass liner
to fit the boat-like bowl of the cachepot without its being wobbly, glue
a piece of sculpted Oasis directly in it, using a water soluble glue which
can be soaked out when you want the container for another purpose.
A piece of Oasis two inches wide, four inches long, and two and one-half
inches high can be shaped with an ordinary knife to fill the bowl and
leave one inch above its rim.

The Assembly

This oval bouquet can be viewed from all sides and is treated like a
back-to-back arrangement. Instead of constantly turning the container
as you insert the flowers, place all of one kind of plant material on
one side, turn the cachepot, and repeat the pattern for all but the
central fan on the other side. Inspect the ends to make sure that you
have not neglected them.

Pink cockscomb is used to shape the arrangement and provide depth
more than it is to play a principal part in the final display. Actually very
little of it will be visible in the completed work, but the color must
blend with the other shades of pink. Use seven pieces to make a fan
across the Oasis, from one end of the container to the other. Start with
the center piece whose tip is nine inches from the table top, and complete the fan by working first to the left and then to the right of the
already placed pieces. Those at the ends of the boat-like bowl are inserted horizontally and project two inches beyond the bowl's rim. Now
place two just over the broad rim of the container between the two pieces
at the ends. These project beyond the rim by one and one-half inches.
Make two rows, each of two pieces of cockscomb, between the top of the
fan and the row at the rim. Repeat all but the fan on the other side.
Now check the profile to make sure that the cockscomb does not bulge
out in the center. Remember that you, for now, are constructing a tent-
like structure.

Place the clusters of large-flowered green hydrangea between the
pieces of cockscomb, but allow them to come up and out about one

and one-half inches beyond them. Start with the fan, then move to the rim of the cachepot and finally fill in holes in the central mass. Turn the container and repeat all but the fan on the other side.

Sort the pink strawflowers by shade and size. Use the smallest and lightest one at the center top of the arrangement, the largest ones as the focal points in the center, and the darker ones near the rim of the container. All of them come out a little more than the hydrangea. Place one in the center of the fan with its tip eleven inches from the table. Make an irregular row of four above the rim of the container and place one on either side of center about halfway up the arrangement. Repeat all but the top flower on the other side.

The pink African daisies come out one inch farther than the large strawflowers. Put one spike in the center of the fan with its tip eleven and one-half inches from the table. With four others, complete the fan, making sure that the spikes at the ends of the bowl are inserted horizontally and project two inches beyond the rim. Make a very irregular row over the rim of the bowl with five flower spikes, the center one jutting three inches beyond the rim. Insert three spikes of daisies across the middle of the bouquet. Repeat the rows on the other side.

The pink pepper berries are wired like most flower spikes but they have the effect of sprays. Reserve the longer sprays with natural curves for use over the rim of the cachepot. Use seven sprays for the fan. Put one, whose tip is ten and one-half inches from the table, in the center of the fan and horizontally insert one over the rim of the bowl at either end. Complete the fan by inserting a spike to the left and to the right of the center one, and then insert a spike to the left and to the right of these. Make an irregular row of five at the rim of the cachepot between the sprays that go over the ends and a row of three across the middle. Repeat all but the fan on the other side.

Five spikes of pink amaranths make still another fan with the tip of the center one twelve inches from the table. Use four spikes for an irregular row above the rim of the container and insert three across the middle of the arrangement.

The clusters of small-flowered green hydrangea come out a little farther than the amaranth spikes and add a light and airy feeling. Place one cluster near the tallest amaranth and make an irregular row of three about one inch above the rim of the cachepot. Insert a cluster on either side of center about halfway up the arrangement. Repeat the pattern on the other side.

Starting at the center of the fan, insert a delicate spike of pink snapdragons with its tip fourteen inches from the table top. This is the highest point in the arrangement. With four additional spikes, complete the fan, allowing the spikes at the ends to jut out beyond the pepper berries. Make an irregular row of three spikes above the rim of the cachepot and insert a spike on either side of the center about halfway up the arrangement. The last five spikes will project out about three inches farther than the African daisies. Repeat all but the fan on the other side.

Finally, place the sprays of maidenhair fern for an additional light touch. These come out almost, but not quite, as far as the snapdragon spikes. Use seven in the fan, three in a row over the container's rim, and two about halfway up the arrangement. Repeat all but the fan on the other side.

Step back and walk around the bouquet. Insert small pieces of fern wherever you see a hole or a thin spot.

Cut Flowers From A Summer Garden

See color pages for illustration.

The Paris porcelain vase contains a traditional half-arrangement of cut flowers which pick up or complement the colors of its decoration. Even though the bouquet seems light and summery, it has many of the characteristics of the buxom bouquets of the eighteenth century. There are several fans of flowers, spikes, and fern and a central mass composed primarily of larger and somewhat heavier flowers from a summer garden.

A reasonably large room is required for the arrangement, which is twenty-three inches high and wide, but it is too delicate for paneling or heavy furniture. Queen Anne or French provincial surroundings seem most compatible.

Pink petunia—Three blossoms on stems with leaves.
Pale lavender ageratum—Seven long stems.
Pink zinnia—Four blossoms.
Red-orange dahlia—One blossom.
Yellow daisy—Ten blossoms.
Pink rose—Five blossoms, two with buds.
Pink snapdragon—Seven natural spikes.
Dianthus—Eleven to fifteen lacey blossoms.
Blue salvia—Thirteen natural spikes.
Loosestrife—Ten natural spikes.
Maidenhair fern—Eleven sprays.
Bachelor's buttons—Four blossoms.

The Assembly

The seven and one-half inch vase flares to five and one-half inches at the top, providing excellent support for the flowers near the rim that project straight out or hang down a bit. Since the oval mouth of the vase measures only two inches by one and one-half inches it cannot hold many leaves or heavy flowers, but it does keep the flowers in position. Fill the vase with water.

Start the assembly with three pink petunias and their leaves. They curve with the shape of the container to help in outlining the final bouquet, and their leaves provide a base to hold other flowers whose stems will be stripped. Place one petunia in the center of the vase, about two inches above its rim. Put one on either side of it, but a little lower.

With five pieces of pale lavender ageratum, make a fan across the back of the container. Start with the tallest and straightest stem whose tip is eighteen inches from the table. Place one piece between the center petunia and each of the lower ones.

Insert a pink zinnia to the right of the center petunia and one just above each of the two pieces of ageratum at the front of the bouquet. Put one to the left and a little lower than the center petunia.

Put a red-orange dahlia over the rim of the vase, a little to the right of center.

Make a fan of five yellow daisies across the back, starting with a small blossom in the center that stands twelve inches from the table. Use the other five daisies to fill in open spaces in the central mass of the arrangement.

The pink roses surround the center petunia. Place one slightly above and to the left of the petunia and another above and to the left of the first rose. Insert a tight bud directly above the petunia and a rose with a bud above and to the right of the tight bud. Put another rose with a bud to the right of the petunia.

Place the tallest and straightest pink snapdragon in the center back of the arrangement, with its tip twenty-three inches from the table. It will become the center of a fan. Select two curved spikes to hang over the container's flare at the lower left and lower right. Now with four spikes and working first to the left and then to the right, complete the fan by inserting the snapdragons between the center spike and those hanging over the flare.

Carefully sort and place the lacey white dianthus so their natural curves conform to the shape of the container. Place the tallest and straightest to the left of the center snapdragon spike. Insert a few in the top half of the fan, but lower than the other flowers in the fan.

With thirteen spikes of blue salvia, make still another fan at about the same height as the snapdragon fan. Be sure that the end pieces come over the container's flare.

Ten spikes of purple loosestrife make still another fan. Starting just to the left and to the right of the center snapdragon, make a fan that is as high or a bit higher than the snapdragon one, but do not carry it down to the container's flare.

Now step back and walk around the bouquet so you can see it from every angle. Add a few more dianthus if you think the bouquet needs more light touches. If it needs more to hang over the ends, insert some yellow daisies or snapdragon spikes.

To give the bouquet a soft and airy look, add some maidenhair fern. Insert it in the back of the fan and allow it to come up and out about as far as the loosestrife.

Finally, add the brilliant blue bachelor's buttons that are to be the focal points of the bouquet. Place one over the rim of the vase to the right of the dahlia and one just to the left of the petunia in the center of the arrangement. The others go above and to the right and left of that petunia.

Peonies in a Delft Bowl

Springlike Cornucopias

A Bouquet for the Harvest Season

Roses in a Pewter Bowl

Cut Flowers from a Summer Garden

A Yellow and Blue Bouquet in a Delft Brick

A Cachepot of Pinks

A Posy Holder of Everlastings

A Posy Holder of Everlastings

See color pages for illustration.

Both the container and the stuffed bouquet reflect the tastes of the flower arrangers of the colonial South. The five-finger posy holder was first created for Queen Mary (1662–1694), an avid lover of flowers, and soon became popular in England. Together with many of the colonists' favorite flowers, this container was imported at least into Williamsburg where the ladies used it to make fan-shaped arrangements of fresh and dried flowers of many different colors and kinds of plant materials.

The traditional half-arrangement is quite formal and sturdy, requiring a large and not too delicate room as well as a backdrop of some kind. Magnolia leaves, so popular in the South of that time, add considerably to the formality of the bouquet. It seems much lighter and airier if the fan is made of goldenrod or fern. In either case, it can be used on a mantle or on a table against a wall and is particularly attractive on a card table with the back raised.

The finished arrangement is twenty inches high and wide.

Magnolia leaves—Thirteen leaves of various sizes, treated in glycerine and water, wired, and taped to the bottom of the wire.

Red cockscomb—Twelve small heads or pieces broken from larger heads, wired in clusters measuring two and one-half inches in diameter.

Cinquefoil—Thirty-six clusters of leaves and buds, wired into eighteen spikes of two each.

Yellow yarrow—Ten small heads or pieces broken from larger heads, wired into clusters measuring one and one-half inches in diameter.

Large white (cream) strawflowers—Thirteen blossoms, wired.

White African daisies—Eighteen blossoms, some with buds, wired.

Miniature red strawflowers—Ten deep red blossoms, wired.

Yellow immortelle—Small clusters of blossoms broken from large heads and wired into fourteen spikes or clusters of about ten blossoms each.

Orange amaranths—Twenty-two blossoms wired into eleven spikes of two each.

Blue statice—Nineteen long natural clusters or spikes made of pieces broken from smaller natural clusters, wired.

Goldenrod—Thirteen spikes made of three or four side shoots, wired.

Blue salvia—Nineteen spikes made of three to five natural spikes, wired.

Petticoat lace—Eleven pieces broken from natural sprays, wired.

Small yellow strawflowers—Twenty to twenty-five blossoms, wired into ten spikes of two or three each.

Pink African daisies—Twenty-four to thirty daisies, wired into eleven spikes of two or three blossoms.

Large white floral buttons—Sixteen spikes of five buttons.

Plume grass—Nineteen to twenty-three spikes of grass made of side shoots, wired.

Preparing the Container

The white posy holder or finger vase of Leeds-type Wedgwood looks a bit like an outstretched china hand on a pedestal. Paintings of the period and modern photographs suggest that these containers hold the flowers in place better than a completely open mouth would, but few people seem able to use them without getting a separated look in the finished product whether they are filled with sand for dried flowers or water for fresh ones. With the use of a modern device, Oasis, the spirit of the eighteenth century bouquets can be kept without the rather unfortunate breaks in the floral mass.

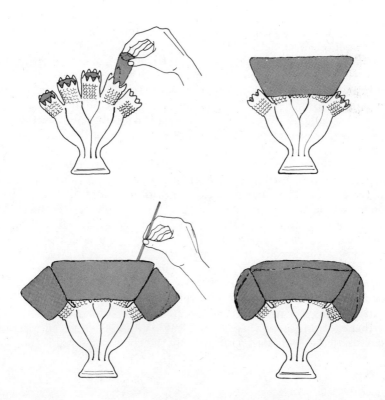

The stuffed bouquet will be top heavy if the container is not weighted. Fill it with sand to within two inches of the top of the fingers. Cut five rectangles of Oasis that are a little larger than the finger openings and are two inches long. Trim these just enough to make a tight fit in the fingers and push them in as far as you can. Trim off the ends of the Oasis so that it is level with the rims of the fingers. Now cut a block of Oasis in half the lengthwise way. You now have two pieces which are nine inches long, two inches wide, and three inches thick. Make an impression of the three center fingers on the bottom of one of those pieces by rolling the Oasis back and forth across the finger openings. Scoop out about one inch or one and one-half inches at the impressions of the finger openings. Fit the carved-out piece over the three center fingers and trim the ends of the Oasis as you would to make a mitered corner. This will allow the pieces to extend over the two outer fingers, angle off, and make a fan-like structure for the arrangement. Cut the other lengthwise piece of Oasis in half and carve out a finger hole in each. Fit the three pieces on the fingers and carve the Oasis to make a fan-like shape with a one inch hangover at either end and a one-half inch hangover in front and in back of the fingers. Round off all of the square corners. Push floral picks into the Oasis over the fingers and through the Oasis stuffed into them. This will secure the fan to the fingers.

The Assembly

Begin the arrangement by making a fan of magnolia leaves across the back of the half circle of Oasis. You may purchase already wired magnolia leaves from dried flower suppliers. If you are going to prepare your own, cut off all but one-half inch of the natural stems which are usually thick and brittle and often crooked. Lay a long wire along the short stem so one end goes half way up the back of the leaf and the other end extends well beyond the leaf's natural stem. Start taping the natural stem and the wire together at the base of the leaf, and continue taping to the end of the wire.

Do not try to insert the leaves, or any other plant materials into the fingers. Insert all materials in the half circle of Oasis. The tallest and largest leaf goes in the center of the fan, with its tips twenty inches from the top of the table. Using pairs of smaller and smaller leaves, insert one just to the left and one just to the right of the already placed leaves. The leaves are increasingly angled out to produce a fan. Those toward the ends of the fan are smaller and come forward in the Oasis. If the heavy leaves tend to slip in the Oasis, put a drop of cement on the end of the wire before inserting it. If you find that the wires seem too weak, use two and tape to the bottom of them.

Place a piece of red cockscomb in front of the center leaf of the fan so that its tip is at the base of the leaf. With six additional pieces of cockscomb and working first to the left and then to the right, complete a cockscomb fan in front of but lower than the fan of leaves. Place another piece of cockscomb about halfway between the center leaf and the rim of the center finger. Put another piece above it and to the right of center and one below it and to the left of center to make a diagonal line across the central mass of the arrangement. Now cross that diagonal line by placing a piece above and to the left of the center one and another below and to its right.

Intersperse the clusters of moss green cinquefoil among the pieces of cockscomb, starting with the fan and moving to the central mass.

In placing the yellow yarrow, be sure that the heads face out, *not* up. You will have to bend the wires of many. Follow the pattern you used in placing the cockscomb. Make a smaller fan in front of and a little below the cockscomb fan and then form crossed diagonal lines across the central mass.

Place one of the smaller cream strawflowers in front of the fan's center leaf so that its tip is fifteen inches from the table. Horizontally insert four of the largest flowers just above the rim of the posy holder. Make an irregular row of four strawflowers below the single flower at the top and another irregular row of four between that row and the one at the rim of the container. Check the profile to make sure that the arrangement is not bulging in the middle.

Put a white African daisy a little above and to the right of the top strawflower and another above and to its left. Make an irregular row of seven flowers at the rim of the posy holder, a row of four blossoms below the white daisies at the top of the arrangement, and a row of five between that row and the one at the rim.

Place a small deep red strawflower to the left of and to the right of center so their tops are sixteen inches from the table. Make an irregular row of four blossoms above the rim of the container and another row of four across the middle of the central mass.

Put a spike of yellow immortelle blossoms in the fan of cockscomb and cinquefoil on either side of the center leaf. With six more spikes and working first on one side and then on the other, continue the fan over the ends of the posy holder. Remember that the fan comes forward on the Oasis near the rim of the container. Place a spike on either side of the center finger near its rim. Make an irregular row of four spikes across the middle of the central mass.

Starting in the center of the fan again, place an orange amaranth spike so that its tip is sixteen inches from the table. Using four more spikes, complete another fan. Then make an irregular row of three above the rim of the container and another row of three across the middle of the central mass.

Blue statice is used as a spike in both the fan and the central mass. Start in the center of the fan with a piece of statice whose tip is eighteen inches from the table. With eight additional spikes, working first on one side and then on the other, complete another fan. The statice spikes at the ends of the fan are seven inches from the table.

Five spikes make an irregular row at the rim of the posy holder and five more are zig-zagged across the middle of the central mass.

The goldenrod spikes come out farther than those made of statice. Use five in the fan with the tip of the center one eighteen inches from the table. Make an irregular row of three above the rim of the posy holder. Five more make a very irregular row across the middle of the central mass. The goldenrod in the central mass comes out one and one-half inches farther than the statice.

The center spike of blue salvia in the fan is a little over eighteen inches from the table and there are four spikes on either side of it. Five spikes make an irregular row near the rim of the holder and five more make a very irregular row a little over half way up the central mass. These come out about one and one-half inches farther than the big strawflowers.

Use eleven pieces of petticoat lace in the fan. The center piece is seventeen inches from the table. Bring the petticoat forward on the Oasis as you get closer to the rim of the posy holder and allow the tips of these to come out beyond the large strawflowers by two inches.

Now to add brightness to the arrangement, insert spikes of small yellow strawflowers. Place one in the center of the fan with its tip fifteen inches from the table. Make an irregular row of six near the base of the arrangement and insert three across the central mass.

Place seven of the pink African daisies in the fan and zig-zag four across the central mass.

To add lightness to the bouquet, insert the spikes of white floral buttons. Use seven in the fan, with the center one eighteen inches from the table. Nine make a zig-zagged row across the central mass.

Finally, to add softness, make a fan of plume grass immediately in front of the magnolia leaves. Allow these to come up almost but not quite, so far as the leaves.

If the posy holder is to be placed in front of a mirror or where the back is even partially exposed, it must be finished off. The simplest way to do this is with a series of magnolia leaf fans that become smaller and smaller, though the back might also be covered with sprays of goldenrod or German statice.

Cut off any wires that have come through the Oasis and are sticking out the back. Then, with the back of the arrangement facing you, make a series of smaller and smaller leaf fans that face you. Be sure that none of the leaf tips are visible from the front of the arrangement and that there are enough fans to cover the Oasis and all wires. If you do not have enough small leaves for the lower fans, simply trim some of the larger ones with ordinary scissors.

Springlike Cornucopias

See color pages for illustration.

The pair of off-white Leeds' pottery horns are filled with fern, leaves, and flowers in such soft and muted tones that even these reasonably large stuffed arrangements seem delicate and lacey. Eighteenth century flower arrangers used wall pockets in many sizes and shapes, some with intricate decorations. Those in the shape of horns, called cornucopias, were hung in pairs, often on either side of a mantle with their curled ends pointed toward each other. They are especially attractive with a mirror between them over a dining room side board.

In the number and order of introduction into *each* horn.

Cinquefoil—Twenty-two clusters of leaves and unopened buds, wired singly unless they seem too thin.

White African everlastings—Twenty-three to twenty-five blossoms, wired singly or with a bud above an open flower.

Large pink strawflowers—Eight, wired singly.

Blue hydrangea—Seven or eight one and one-half inch clusters of very young blossoms and buds, broken from large clusters, wired.

Spirea leaves—Twelve to fifteen branches of glycerine-treated leaves, taken from the tips of the natural branches, wired.

Petticoat lace—Thirteen sprays, one and one-half inches in diameter, broken from the large natural sprays, wired.

English or shasta daisies—Five, wired singly.

Yellow daisies—Five, wired singly.

Yellow statice—Twelve elongated clusters, wired singly.

Delphinium—Five spikes of light blue blossoms, wired, and several side flowers, wired singly.

Pink spirea—Three clusters, wired.

Maidenhair fern—Seven pieces broken from natural sprays, wired.

Miniature floral buttons—Nine to twelve spikes of fifteen to twenty individual buttons, wired with as long natural stems as possible.

Feverfew—Three to five natural clusters, wired.

Preparing the Containers

Fill the horns with small pieces of Oasis and push it down with a pencil or floral pick. The Oasis should come to within one and one-half inches of the top of the back which is lower than the front. Do not try to substitute sand for this because it will make the containers too heavy to hang on many walls. Next cut a solid piece of Oasis that measures two inches by five inches by three inches. With a knife carve the ends to follow the lines of the top of the horn and the bottom into a V-like shape that will fit into the opening and leave one and one-half or two inches of Oasis above the back of the container. Push this piece into the horn as tightly as you can. Anchor the solid piece to the packed broken pieces with floral picks and clip off the exposed ends of the picks. They must go through the solid piece and well into the broken pieces.

The Assembly

Whenever you are arranging pairs of bouquets, it is essential that you do them together. Place a flower in one container and then put a similar flower in a comparable position in the other. The curls of the cornucopias must be facing each other as you work, if the finished arrangements are to match. If you place a flower on the inside of the curl in one container, the same kind of flower must be placed on the inside of the curl of the other. A flower that is to the right of center in the horn on the left will be matched by one to the left of center in the other.

These containers will not stand alone and it is not possible to arrange in them when they are lying on the work table or hanging on a wall. The best technique seems to be to insert the curled ends into blocks of Oasis and then put them in front of you as they will be viewed when they are hanging on a wall. The instructions given here are for one horn.

With nine spikes of moss green cinquefoil, make a fan across the back of the Oasis. Place a spike in the center back so that its tip is eight inches above the back rim of the cornucopia. Then, working to the left and to the right of the already placed spikes, complete the fan. The spikes that go over the sides of the horn project two and one-half inches beyond it. Remember that these horns will be placed against a wall, so their backs must be kept flat. With eight more spikes of cinquefoil, make a smaller and lower fan across the middle of the Oasis. Five spikes make an irregular row at the rim of the container to complete the outline of the arrangement.

Now, fill in that outline with white African everlastings, using the buds and smaller flowers at the top and the larger ones near the rim of the container. Use nine flowers to make a fan in front of and about one-half inch lower than the cinquefoil fan. Partially fill the holes between the other pieces of cinquefoil with white everlastings but push them in farther.

Insert the eight pink strawflowers in remaining holes in the central mass of the arrangement. They are not to be included in the fan at the back, but some of them must come over the rim of the horn to break that line. This is especially important since the arrangements will sometimes be viewed from below.

Use the clusters of blue hydrangea to fill any remaining holes in the central mass of the arrangement. Do not place them in the back fan, but some may be placed in front of and below it. Although hydrangea can be hang dried, it will curl more that way than if it is preserved in silica gel. If possible, use gel-preserved hydrangea here.

The branches of spirea leaves are the highest spikes in the fan. The tip of the center spike is twelve inches higher than the back of the cornucopia or three inches higher than the center piece of cinquefoil in that fan. Most of the spirea leaves are used near the top of the bouquet, but a few are inserted throughout to carry their color and texture from the top to the bottom of the arrangement. Those near the rim of the container are to be inserted so they hang over it by about two inches and those in the central mass are inserted in a much more upright position and project out beyond the cinquefoil by about three inches.

The delicate sprays of pink petticoat lace add a light and airy feeling to the bouquet. Use nine in the back fan, but be sure they are no higher than the spirea leaves. Intersperse four sprays in the central mass and allow them to come forward as far as, but no farther than, the branches of leaves.

It would be possible to stop at this point in the arrangement, for the cornucopias are very attractive as they are, with the pink strawflowers as the focal points. In some ways though, this is where the fun really begins. It must have been at times like this that Louise Fisher found "it hard to resist the impulse to add 'just one more'" to her arrangements for the rooms of Colonial Williamsburg.

She might have then gone to her eighteenth century garden and picked some daisies, a few spikes of blue delphinium, some spirea, half dozen or so clusters of the tiny daisy-like feverfew blossoms, and a little fern. I felt compelled to add to these some yellow statice spikes and miniature floral buttons.

For new focal points, insert the English daisies. Put one in the center of the central mass. Place two over the rim of the container, one on either side of its center, and put one above and to the left of the center daisy and one above and to its right.

Place a yellow daisy above the center of the horn's rim. Use four in a zig-zagged row across the middle of the central mass.

With seven elongated clusters of yellow statice, make a fan in front of and below the fans of petticoat lace and spirea leaves. Remember to start with the center cluster and then work first to the left and then to the right of the already-placed clusters. Use five more clusters to make another fan, this one two inches below the first.

Insert five spikes of delphinium in the smaller fan of yellow statice. Insert a few of the individual side blossoms in the central mass.

Place three spikes of pink spirea across the top of the fan. These should be inserted in front of and a little lower than the spirea leaves.

Add seven pieces of maidenhair fern to the back fan. It is about as high as the spirea-leaf fan.

Insert three spikes of miniature floral buttons in the center of the back fan at the same height as the tallest statice fan. Make a very irregular row of five spikes above the rim of the container and insert a single spike just above the center of the central mass.

Finally, insert three to five clusters of feverfew just below the smaller fan of statice.

Now it is probably time to start resisting those impulses to add, add, add.

Possible Substitutions

If you have difficulty in finding petticoat lace, try using instead either pink larkspur or artemisia 'Silver King.' Other larkspur and blue salvia might be used as substitutes for some of the spikey plant materials and, of course, other ferns may be used.

Colorful Twin Miniatures

These Staffordshire cottage vases with embossed cameo fronts are filled with traditional half-arrangements of flowers of many colors and shapes. Some of the more delicate flowers are natural spikes; others are wired into spike-like forms, and the larger flowers make up the central mass. Although the total effect is quite formal, the bouquets are dainty. They might be placed on a narrow mantle, a lady's writing table, or in a powder room. The bouquets are thirteen inches high and eleven inches wide.

In the number and order of introduction into *each* vase.

Red plume celosia—Eleven spikes measuring two to three inches and made of three or four side shoots, wired.

Pink cockscomb—Three clusters, one inch in diameter, wired.

Artemisia 'Silver King'—Fifty-one branches wired into seventeen spikes of three each.

Bloodwort—Nine pieces, wired singly.

Blue hydrangea—Five clusters of four to five flowers broken from large clusters, wired.

White African everlastings—Five, wired singly.

Pink African daisies—Five, wired singly.

Red strawflowers—Seven, wired singly.

Pale yellow African daisies—Five, wired singly.

Blue salvia—Seven spikes, wired singly.

Purple, blue, and pink statice—Three pieces of each color, three-quarters of an inch in diameter, broken from natural clusters, wired.

Yellow immortelle—Twenty-five or thirty blossoms, wired into five spikes of five or six.

Maidenhair fern—Fourteen stems of leaflets, wired, and five to seven one-inch pieces, broken from the tips of the leaves.

Miniature floral buttons—Eighty to ninety buttons, wired into nine spikes of nine to thirteen each.

Preparing the Containers

These tiny vases are four and one-quarter inches high in the front and five inches high at the back. They have small oval openings that measure one inch by one and one-half inches. To provide a larger area into which to insert the flowers, cut a piece of Oasis two inches long, two inches high, and one and one-half inches thick. Taper the bottom one inch of Oasis so it will fit into the flare of the vases and the very bottom will go into the small hole. Make a similar piece of Oasis for the twin vase. Fill the containers with sand up to that hole and insert the carved Oasis into the top, pushing it in firmly without crumbling the Oasis or cracking the fragile china. One inch of Oasis will stand above the highest part of the container's rim. Put a floral pick through the Oasis and into the sand. Trim off the exposed end of the floral pick.

The Assembly

When working with pairs of containers, place one piece of plant material in one container and a similar piece in a comparable position in its pair.

Begin by making a back fan of red plume celosia with the tip of the center spike twelve inches from the table. The tips of those hanging over the sides of the container should project four inches from the center of the opening. Remember to place a piece of plant material in the center of the back of the Oasis, a piece over either end, and then finish the fan by placing a piece to the left and then to the right of the center spike and then to the left and the right of the already placed materials, until you reach those over the flare.

The small clusters of pink cockscomb are used to provide body and depth for the central mass of the arrangements. Place one cluster on either side of center just above the rim of the vase and a third between these, but two and one-half inches higher than the two at the rim.

With eleven pieces of artemisia, fill in the plume celosia fan. Most of these are inserted at the same heights and angles as the plumes, but add six more a little lower and just in front of the celosia fan.

Now make a smaller fan of nine spikes of bloodwort in front of and about one and one-half inches lower than the celosia-artemisia fan.

Place three clusters of blue hydrangea above the rim of the vase. Between these, but three inches higher, insert two more clusters.

Next place several kinds of flowers in the central mass where there is to be a variety of colors and shapes. It is here that there is a danger of a bulge developing. With the addition of each new kind of plant material, turn the container and check the profile. Keep in mind the diagonal line of a right-angle triangle and remember that the larger and darker blossoms of each color and variety go near the rim of the vase. With these cautions in mind, place five white African everlastings, five pink African daisies, seven small red strawflowers, and five yellow African daisies in the central mass. It will get very full with these additions. If you find that you cannot get the wires in where you want to place the blossoms, you may have to either use tweezers to insert the flowers or even glue a few to the cockscomb base.

Now make still another fan. This one is of blue salvia spikes and is placed lower than the fan of celosia and artemisia.

Next make a multi-colored fan of nine pieces of statice—three each of purple and blue and pink, all distributed evenly across the fan and placed one inch lower than the celosia and artemisia fan.

Insert five spikes of immortelle blossoms at the outer edge of the central mass and the inner edge of the series of fans.

At the very back of the arrangement, make a new fan of nine pieces of maidenhair fern. This fan will be higher than any other. Insert five additional pieces of fern in the central mass, allowing them to project up and out one inch farther than any of the flowers. The pieces of fern in the body may be glued into place if the Oasis is too crowded with wires. Just put a drop of glue on the stem, push it well into the mass of flowers, and hold it in place for a minute.

Finally, make a fan of the nine spikes of miniature floral buttons just in front of the fan of maidenhair. The floral buttons do not come out quite as far as the fern.

Harmonious Bouquets

A limited amount of color contrast, the absence of stylized lines and back fans, and a larger proportion of compositions that can be viewed from all sides distinguish the harmonious bouquets from those in the more traditional style. The harmonious ones are also characterized by a wide range in the degree of formality of the containers used and by a close affinity between the plant materials and the flower holders.

Color contrast is quite subdued in the collection of money and pink strawflowers and in the alabaster container of white and beige plant materials. Although several of the arrangements contain many different kinds of flowers, the number of colors used is small. The pâté mold is stuffed with many plant materials in only silver and rose to lavender; the very full harvest arrangement contains just the more subtle autumnal colors. The Wedgwood vase holds blue and white flowers, and the arrangement in the silver bowl is red, white, and blue.

All of the harmonious bouquets, except the one in the cricket cage, can be viewed from any direction. Even the filigree lid of the cage, which is visible from one side, is attractive. Five of the other arrangements are all-around compositions and two are oblong with central fans.

The containers used in this collection of arrangements run the gamut from crude to very formal. The unglazed terra-cotta jug is really just a more pleasantly shaped flower pot. At the formal end of the continuum, there is a silver bowl and a fluted porcelain vase with gold trim. Among those falling between the crude and the formal are a brown pitcher, a brass cricket cage, an aluminum pâté mold, and a Wedgwood vase.

The plant materials in harmonious bouquets show a special affinity for their containers. When the Castleford bowl is placed in the light, both it and the coins of the money plant have an almost irridescent sheen, and the brown and orange marigolds reflect both the color and the luster of the milk pitcher. Blue and white flowers precisely reproduce the colors of the Wedgwood vase, and six white and gray plant materials somehow enhance the silvery tone of the aluminum mold.

Ingredients for the arrangements are given in the order in which they are used.

A Bouquet for the Harvest Season

See color pages for illustration.

Autumnal colors make the harvest arrangement an ideal centerpiece for a Thanksgiving table. The yellow and gold flowers are bright and colorful and tend to complement the shiny brass mold. Green-brown leaves and glossy wood roses contribute a warm and woodsy feeling to what remains a formal and elegant bouquet. It seems perfect for a large rectangular table in the dining room or library of a country home, but would also be effective on a room divider in a more contemporary setting. The arrangement is twenty inches wide and fifteen inches high.

Golden crested cockscomb—Twenty-nine pieces, one to one and one-half inches in diameter, either small heads or pieces broken from large heads, wired.

Yellow yarrow—Twenty clusters, one and one-half inches in diameter, either small heads or pieces broken from large heads, wired.

Cinquefoil—Ninety pieces of leaves and unopened buds, wired into thirty clusters of three.

Laurel leaves—Seven natural sprays of glycerine-treated leaves, each with about five leaves, wired.

White African daisies—Thirty-five or forty blossoms, twelve large ones wired singly and smaller flowers wired into sixteen spikes with the smaller flower above the larger.

Large white strawflowers—Twenty-eight, wired singly.

Small orange strawflowers—Seventy-five, wired into thirty spikes of two or three.

Yellow African daisies—Forty or fifty blossoms, wired into nineteen spikes of two or three.

Wood roses—Twenty-two natural clusters of two or three "roses," wired.

Yellow immortelle—Thirty clusters of five to eight blossoms broken from large natural clusters, wired.

Orange amaranths—Twenty-eight spikes of two or three blossoms.

Coppery plume celosia—Side shoots, wired into thirty-two three-inch spikes.

Goldenrod—Thirty spikes, three or three and one-half inches long, made of side shoots, wired.

Wheat—Sixteen spikes of two or three heads, wired.

Laurel leaves—Twelve natural sprays of glycerine-treated leaves, wired.

Calendula—Twelve blossoms, wired individually.

Rusty dock—Five long side shoots, wired individually.

Preparing the Container

Use a liner in the brass mold so the arrangement can be removed when the container needs to be polished or when it is needed for a summertime bouquet. Either a milk carton or a papier mache liner will fit into the eleven by three inch mold. Cut a piece of Oasis that will snugly fit into the liner and glue it into place. Since one piece is not high enough to rise one inch above the rim of the mold, cut another to be placed on the top of the first. Push three wooden floral picks through both pieces of Oasis to be sure the top layer does not slip. Attach the filled liner to the brass mold with floral clay.

The Assembly

Because this is a long bouquet that is to be viewed from all sides, use the rules for a back-to-back arrangement. Except for the plant materials in the fan, place all of one kind of flower on one side of the arrangement, then turn the container and repeat the pattern on the other side. Check the ends of the arrangement to make sure they are not being neglected before beginning work with the next variety.

Begin the assembly by placing the golden cockscomb. It is the heaviest material, provides a good base for the other plant materials, and gives depth to the final arrangement. The first piece goes in the exact center of the Oasis with its tip eleven inches from the top of the table. Horizontally insert a piece over either end of the container, allowing it to project three and one-half inches beyond the rim of the container. With six more pieces, complete the fan by placing one to the left and one to the right of the center clump of cockscomb. Continue working first to the left and then to the right of the previously placed pieces of cockscomb until you reach those horizontally inserted over the ends of the container. Horizontally insert six pieces in an irregular row at the rim of one of the broad sides of the brass mold and jutting out about one inch beyond it. Then, at a forty-five degree angle insert four in an irregular row between those at the rim and those in the fan. Turn the container and repeat the two rows on the other side. Check the profile from either end to make sure that cockscomb does not bulge out in the middle. Imagine a diagonal line drawn from the tip of the top center piece of cockscomb to those at its rim.

Keep that imaginary line in mind as you place the heads of yellow yarrow. Insert ten pieces of yarrow among the cockscomb on one side. Turn the container and repeat the pattern on the other side.

Working in three more-or-less irregular rows—one near the fan, one near the container's rim, and one between those—place the clusters of cinquefoil among the big and bulky pieces of cockscomb and yarrow. Now the basic shape of the arrangement has been outlined and there is a base of cockscomb, yarrow, and cinquefoil. From now on all the flowers will come up and out from that base.

With seven sprays of laurel leaves, make a fan whose center spray is fifteen inches from the table. Horizontally insert a spray over either end of the brass mold and allow them to project six inches beyond the rim and droop over it a bit. Complete the fan by working first to the left and then to the right of the center spray and then to the left and to the right of the already placed sprays.

Use the smaller white African daisies near the top of the arrangement and the larger ones near the bottom, allowing them to come up and out a little farther than the cockscomb and yarrow. Place three in the top third of the fan, make an irregular row of six at the rim of the container, and zig-zag five across the middle. Repeat the pattern on the other side.

Follow a similar pattern in placing the large white strawflowers, but allow them to come out a bit more than the African daisies.

The spikes of two orange strawflowers go near the top of the arrangement and those of three go near the bottom. All of these come out a bit farther than the large white strawflowers, but must not hide them. Make three irregular rows of two spikes near the top, seven near the rim, and six in between.

All of the large flowers are now in place. Except for the fan of leaves, the arrangement now looks a bit like half a football. Continue building the height and fullness of the arrangement with the small yellow African daisies. Place one in the center of the fan, with its tip twelve inches from the table. It is now the tallest flower, not leaf, in the bouquet. With four more daisy spikes, complete the fan. Make an irregular row of four above the rim of the mold and zig-zag three more across the middle. Repeat the pattern for all but the fan on the other side.

Wood roses are the major focal points so they must come out farther than anything else now in the arrangement, but they must not hide the large white strawflowers, which are the secondary focal points. Make an irregular row of six or seven clusters of roses above the rim of the mold and a row of four or five clusters about three inches below the yellow African daisies in the center of the fan.

Now begin working with the more spikey materials. Remember to pay particular attention to the fan with these, but do not neglect the body of the arrangement and the rim of the container. Place four immortelle spikes below the fan and make an irregular row of five at the rim of the container. Zig-zag six across the middle. Repeat the pattern on the other side and inspect the ends.

Make a fan of seven spikes of orange amaranths, starting with the center spike and working first to the left and then to the right of the already placed spikes. Four more make an irregular row at the rim of the container and another three go across the middle of the arrangement.

With nine spikes of plume celosia make a fan in front of and a little lower than the fan of laurel leaves. Place five in an irregular row over the rim of the container and insert one on either side of the center of the arrangement. These come out two inches farther than the cockscomb and yarrow base. Repeat the fan and the rows on the other side.

Make a fan of seven spikes of goldenrod in front of the laurel-leaf fan and slightly higher than the fan of plume celosia. Place five spikes in an irregular row over the rim of the brass mold and insert three across the broad middle of the arrangement. The spikes in the rows come out about three inches farther than the yarrow or one inch farther than the plume celosia. Repeat the whole pattern on the other side.

Insert two spikes of wheat below and on either side of the center of the fan. Place three about one inch above the rim of the container and three more across the middle of the arrangement. The spikes over the rim and in the middle come out about as far as the plume celosia.

Now, return to the sprays of laurel leaves. Place one below the fan, at the center top of the central mass. Put one over the center of the rim of the mold and one at either front corner so they fall over the mold. Insert one on either side of the center of the arrangement. Repeat this pattern on the other side.

To return to the central mass, place a single calendula blossom below the center of the fan. Distribute three above the rim of the mold and place one on either side of center in the middle of the arrangement.

Finally, insert the five pieces of rusty dock across the central fan.

A Castleford Bowl of Muted Tones

The combination of delicate pink strawflowers with the irridescent coins of money, sprays of pink petticoat lace, and beige grasses make a light and subtle arrangement. Similar bouquets must have appeared on the tables and sideboards of eighteenth century houses, for all but the petticoat lace, which is native to the Southwest, are known to have been used by the flower arrangers of that time. The oval sugar bowl of off-white pottery with silvery gray embossed bands is also of the eighteenth century, about 1780.

The light and delicate bouquet would be out of place with heavy furniture, but a period room or a contemporary setting of glass and chrome seem quite fitting.

The arrangement is eighteen inches high and wide.

Money (Honesty)—Thirty-two side shoots on their natural stems, each with about five coins, with seeds and outer casings removed.

Large pink strawflowers—Eighteen blossoms, wired singly.

Small pink strawflowers—Twenty-eight blossoms, twelve smaller ones wired singly, sixteen wired into eight spikes of two blossoms each.

Petticoat lace—Seventeen small sprays broken from large natural sprays, wired.

Rattail millet—Sixty heads, wired into twenty spikes of three.

Wheat—Forty-five heads, wired into fifteen spikes of three.

Preparing the Container

The oval bowl is four and one-half inches high and measures six and one-half inches from end to end. Invert it on the top of a block of Oasis to make an impression of the opening. Cut through the block on that line and insert the Oasis in the bowl just far enough to leave one and one-half inches projecting above the rim of the container.

The rules for back-to-back arrangements apply for this oval bouquet. Place all of one kind of plant material on one side, turn the container, and repeat the pattern for all but the fan on the other side. Inspect the ends to make sure they are not too thin before placing the next kind of flower.

The Assembly

Place a piece of money in the center of the Oasis so its tip is fifteen inches from the top of the table. Horizontally insert a piece at either end of the oval bowl and allow them to project five inches beyond its rim. Now, starting from that center piece and working first to the left and then to the right, insert pieces of money to complete a fan between the center piece and those at the ends. Select pieces of money with shorter stems and horizontally insert them in the Oasis at the rim of the container so their tips are three inches beyond it. Fill in between the fan and those at the rim with pieces of money that have shorter and shorter stems as you move from the rim toward the fan. Repeat all but the fan on the other side. You now have a bright, light, and soft mass of shining coins.

Insert two of the large strawflowers near the tall center spike of money but two inches lower than it is and place three across the middle of the arrangement. Push these well into the money. Horizontally insert a strawflower at either end of the container allowing them to project three inches beyond its rim. Three blossoms should be inserted horizontally at the rim of the bowl between those at the ends, but they should be allowed to come out only two inches. Repeat the pattern on the other side, except for those at the ends of the oval. The difference between the lengths of the projections at the ends and on the sides of the bowl maintains the original oval shape.

Place six of the small pink strawflowers in the top half of the bouquet. Put one between and a little above the two large strawflowers near the top of the arrangement and place two just below and outside them. Insert three above and a little to the left of the three blossoms across the middle of the bouquet. Make the small strawflowers appear to be buds on the stems of the large ones. They should project out beyond the big flowers, but by no more than one inch. Place four of the spikes of small strawflowers near the large ones in the bottom half of the arrangement. Turn the container and repeat the pattern on the other side.

Starting at the top center of the arrangement and using seven sprays of petticoat lace, make a fan that goes from one end of the oval to the other and is two to three inches higher than the fan of money. Place two sprays over the rim of the bowl, allowing them to come out beyond the large strawflowers by two and one-half inches. Insert three sprays across the middle of the arrangement. These come out three to three and one-half inches farther than the large strawflowers. Repeat the pattern used in placing the last five sprays on the other side.

Place six spikes of rattail millet in the fan of money and petticoat lace, but avoid the exact center of the fan. The spikes should come out three to four inches farther than the money. Insert a spike of millet over the rim at either end of the container, allowing it to project out seven and one-half inches beyond the rim. Put three spikes over the rim of the side of the bowl in a considerably more upright position than those horizontally inserted at the ends. These should project only six inches beyond the container. Place three spikes across the middle of the bouquet. Repeat the pattern for all but the fan on the other side.

Finally, insert three spikes of wheat in the upper half of the fan, starting with the center piece which should stand eighteen inches from the table. The other pieces in the fan should come out four or five inches farther than the money. Insert two wheat spikes over the rim just to the right and to the left of center and zig-zag four spikes across the middle of the arrangement. Repeat all but the fan on the other side.

Fresh from an August Garden

Any dark corner would be brightened by this all-around arrangement of orange and yellow marigolds and lavender ageratum. The white accents of feverfew and chive blossoms pick up the color of the graceful and elegant china vase with gold accents, and the fuzzy ageratum provides a good contrast in texture to the bold color and shape of the marigolds. The bouquet is eighteen inches high, about thirteen inches wide at the rim of the vase, and fifteen inches wide at its broadest point. It is too tall for a dining table or a mantle and is too tippable for a coffee table, but it would be effective in front of a mirror, on a deep window sill, or in an entry hall.

Lavender ageratum—Fifteen or sixteen stems measuring twelve to sixteen inches, with their leaves.

Large orange and yellow marigolds and zinnias—Thirty-four blossoms, with leaves removed from the lower part of the stems.

Feverfew—Three elongated clusters of seven to ten blossoms.

Oriental chive—Nine clusters.

Boston daisy—Six blossoms, with leaves removed from the lower part of their leaves.

Small orange and brown marigolds—Fifteen blossoms.

The Assembly

Fill the container with water almost to the top. Put twelve pieces of lavender ageratum in the vase, leaving all the leaves on the stems. They will be helpful in keeping the other flowers in position. The ageratum forms a sketchy and loose base for the bouquet. The tallest pieces go in the center of the vase, the shortest at the rim, and the others in between. The tip of the center piece will be eighteen inches from the table, those on the outer edges project about three inches beyond the rim of the vase, and those at the bouquet's widest point, which is between two to three inches above the rim, project five inches beyond the rim.

The orange and yellow marigolds and zinnias are the focal points of the arrangement. Use the smaller blossoms near the top and the larger ones at the base. Place the tallest and smallest marigold in the center of the bouquet with its tip fifteen inches from the table. In a circle around but just below that blossom, place four more flowers. Try to choose those with bent stems so the flowers will face out. These must be pushed well into the ageratum, so the spikes of fuzzy blue flowers project out beyond the marigolds by up to two inches. Make an irregular row of fifteen marigolds and zinnias just above the rim of the vase. With six blossoms, make an irregular row below the circle of four flowers and zig-zag eight around the bouquet above the row at the rim.

Now get up and walk around the arrangement. Fill in any holes you see with delicate pieces of ageratum.

From now on, all the flowers are to come out farther than the marigolds and zinnias but not so far as the ageratum. Evenly distribute three clusters of feverfew blossoms around the rim of the vase.

Make an irregular row of the nine clusters of Oriental chive blossoms just below the middle of the arrangement.

Insert six yellow daisy blossoms in an irregular row just above the middle of the bouquet.

Place the small brown and orange marigolds in three irregular rows. Put three around but lower than the top center marigold. Use seven blossoms in an irregular row above the rim of the container and five in a middle row.

Finally, select small and delicate pieces of ageratum, tearing off some of the side shoots if they seem too heavy for spikes. Insert these wherever there are holes in the bouquet, making sure that they project beyond all but the other ageratum.

Golden Hues in a Cricket Cage

Plant materials of mostly autumnal colors fill the brass filigree container and make a small but elegant arrangement. The rather solid base of cockscomb, African daisies, and strawflowers is relieved by the twisted leaflets of the rich, but light, brown fern and the delicate spikes of goldenrod. The fern and goldenrod seem to reflect the mood of the cut-out cricket cage. Touches of deep rusty red and white accent the combination of yellows and golds.

In the Orient, the songs sung by crickets kept in these cages delight many, especially those who believe crickets are signs of good luck.

The half-arrangement is probably best placed against a wall or some other backdrop even though the raised lid at the back is extremely attractive. The bouquet, which is twelve and one-half inches high and fifteen and one-half inches wide, would be handsome on a shelf in a corner cabinet, on an end table, a desk top, or even in a powder room.

Yellow yarrow—Seven small heads or pieces broken from larger heads, wired into seven one-and-one-half inch clusters.

Rusty red cockscomb—Eight small heads or pieces broken from larger heads, wired into eight two-inch clusters.

Apricot strawflowers—Twelve, wired singly.

White African daisies—Sixteen buds or flowers, wired singly.

Orange amaranths—Eighteen, wired into nine spikes of two blossoms.

Small deep rust strawflowers—Ten, wired singly.

Rusty golden plume celosia—Thirteen spikes made of side shoots and measuring three inches.

Orange 'Old Mexico' zinnias—Five, wired singly.

Goldenrod—Fifty-four side shoots wired in twenty-seven spikes of two.

Fertile leaves of narrow-leaved chain-fern—Nine tips from leaves, measuring four to five and one-half inches.

Preparing the Container

Cut through a block of Oasis to make a circle that will snugly fit into the cage which is almost four and one-half inches in diameter. When you push it into the container, a little over one inch will stand above the rim. Measure three-quarters of an inch in from the center front of the raised Oasis and cut an arc off the Oasis along that line and level with the top of the cricket cage. Then trim off the corners created by the piece removed. Twist the center of a twelve-inch wire around the catch on the container's lid and insert the ends of the wire into the Oasis on either side of the front of the cage to prop the lid up as far as it will go.

The Assembly

Place a piece of yellow yarrow at the back of the Oasis, just in front of the lid and just to the right of center. Its tip should be six and three-quarter inches from the table. Another, just to the left of center at the back, is six inches from the table. Place a head of yarrow in the exact center of the Oasis so it is five and one-half inches high. On either side, where the lid and the rim of the container meet, horizontally insert a piece of yarrow and allow it to jut out over the rim by about one inch. Just to the right and the left of center front, horizontally insert yarrow heads and allow them to come one inch over the edge of the cricket cage.

Put a piece of cockscomb on either side of the yarrow in the center of the Oasis and one just over the rim of the cage in the center front. Place a piece of cockscomb beside or above all of the other yarrow heads except the one just to the right of center at the back.

An apricot strawflower goes near each of the pieces of yarrow that are just off center at the back of the arrangement. Make an irregular row of five above the rim of the container and one row of five blossoms across the middle.

The bud of a white African daisy goes at the center back and stands nine and one-half inches high. Make an irregular row of five of the larger flowers just over the rim of the container. Then, using smaller and smaller flowers, and working up toward the bud at the top, make one row of four, and two rows of three blossoms.

Place a spike of orange amaranths in front of the lid, just to the right of the center back. It stands ten inches high. One not quite so high goes just to the left of the center back. Make an irregular row of four spikes above the rim of the cage and one of three across the middle of the bouquet. These come out a bit farther than the apricot strawflowers and white African daisies.

Two of the deep rust strawflowers are off center near the top of the bouquet, but not quite so high as the tallest spike of amaranths. Make an irregular row of five blossoms above the container's rim and one of three across the middle of the arrangement.

Five celosia spikes form a fan across the back of the arrangement. Their tips come up and out about two inches farther than the white African daisies, and the center spike is ten inches high. Remember that in making a fan you always start with the center spike, then put one to the left and one to the right of the already placed flowers. Insert five celosia spikes above the rim of the cage at about a forty-five degree angle. Place three in the middle of the bouquet at about the same angle.

The orange zinnias are the focal points of the bouquet. Put one just below the center of the central mass, one over the rim at the lower left, and another at the upper right, forming a diagonal line across the central mass. Then cross that line by placing a zinnia in the upper left and one in the lower right of the mass. All of these must come out farther than the African daisies and strawflowers.

Use nine spikes of goldenrod to make another fan across the back of the arrangement, with the tip of the center spike eleven inches from the table. With seven more spikes, make another fan that is in front of and one inch lower than the first. Then make three rows of goldenrod across the central mass of the arrangement. The tips of these come out two inches farther than the strawflowers. Insert four, almost horizontally, over the rim of the cricket cage. Put four in a row just below the center of the central mass in a slightly more upright position and three in a row just above the center, at a still more upright position.

The highest point in the final arrangement is the fern leaf in the center of the back fan. Its tip is twelve and one-half inches from the table. The tips of those at the ends of the fan are five and one-half inches beyond the container's rim.

Zinnias in a Lustre Pitcher

The deep brown, copper lustre pitcher with canary banding is part of an old mush and milk set. All of the plant materials bring out the feeling of the container, and the arrangement complements its shape, color, and texture. The brown zinnias with their orange and gold markings are the focal points and pick up the colors of the pitcher almost perfectly. White floral buttons brighten the arrangement and the petticoat lace lightens what might otherwise be a rather heavy and dark composition.

The pitcher is not so crude as a crockery or earthenware container, but it seems to require an informal setting. A wooden kitchen table seems particularly appropriate. The arrangement is thirteen inches tall and twelve inches wide.

Bloodwort—Forty to forty-five stems of seed pods, wired only for height.

'Navajo' or 'Persian' zinnias—Thirty blossoms with one-inch stems, the larger ones to be used in the bottom half of the arrangement, wired; the smaller ones for the top of the bouquet, given false bloodwort stems.

Bloodwort stems—Fifteen stems to be used as false stems for the zinnias in the top of the arrangement.

Large floral buttons—Fifty to sixty buttons, wired into fifteen spikes of three or four each.

Petticoat lace—Twenty-two fanlike sprays, broken from the natural sprays and measuring four and one-half inches by three and one-quarter inches, wired.

Hairy beard-tongue seed pods—Fifteen natural stems of seed pods.

Preparing the Container

Cut a piece of Oasis just large enough to fill the three and one-quarter inch opening of the five inch high pitcher and wedge it into the opening far enough to leave one or one and one-half inches of Oasis above the rim.

The Assembly

Place a piece of bloodwort in the center of the Oasis so its tip is eleven inches from the table and make a row around the rim of the container that horizontally juts out by about an inch. Now fill in between the top and the bottom with enough pieces of bloodwort to make a loose cone shape that is thicker at the bottom.

Because this is a rather loose bouquet, wires of the flowers at the top would show. To prepare stems for the smaller zinnias that go at the top of the arrangement, put a drop of Duco cement on the end of a blood-wort stem and insert that in the hollow stem of a zinnia. Place one flower in the center of the bloodwort cone, with its tip twelve inches from the table. Next make an irregular row of twelve wired flowers around the rim of the pitcher. Insert these horizontally, letting them come out one-half to two and one-half inches over the rim and bend the wires so the flowers appear to droop a bit. Make a row of ten flowers above the row at the rim. These jut out one inch farther from the rim than the drooping ones. This helps duplicate the shape of the container in the arrangement. Make another irregular row of seven zinnias between the lower rows and the blossoms at the top center of the arrangement. These come out one and one-half to two inches farther than the bloodwort. Remember to keep turning the container as you work and that all plant materials are inserted in increasingly more upright positions as you move from the rim to the top of the bouquet.

Place two spikes of white floral buttons near the center top of the bouquet and allow them to rise above the bloodwort by one or one and one-half inches. Insert six spikes a little less than horizontally just above the rim of the pitcher. Insert the others in a more upright position to make an irregular row around the middle of the bouquet.

The center spray of petticoat lace will be the highest point of the ar-rangement. It is thirteen inches from the table. Insert six sprays of petticoat around the rim of the pitcher and allow them to jut out about five inches beyond it. Every other one of these should droop down. The rest of the petticoat should be interspersed among the zinnias between the top flower and the bottom row. All of these come out about three inches farther than the zinnias.

Finally, place the stems of pods. Put two of the tallest and straightest stems near the top center of the arrangement, but not quite so high as the tallest spray of petticoat. Insert six smaller stems in an irregular row above the rim of the pitcher and intersperse seven in an irregular row around the middle of the bouquet.

From White to Beige in Alabaster

The contrast between the soft beige or off-white of the amaranths, the large strawflowers, and the grass with the stark whites of the African everlastings and floral buttons is muted but effective. As a "special occasion" bouquet, it might also be made in a silver bowl, and would be especially appropriate for a wedding or an anniversary. The arrangement will make a grand gift for someone with whose color scheme you are not familiar.

The all-around, stylized bouquet, done in an eighteenth century manner, is particularly versatile both because of its size and the "safe" color scheme. It would be attractive in a living room, a dining room, or a bedroom if the furniture is not too heavy. The fern and the grass give the arrangement a light and delicate feel, and the Florentine alabaster bird bath adds elegance.

The overall measurements are thirteen by thirteen inches.

Golden cockscomb—Thirteen small heads or pieces, one and one-half inches in diameter, broken from larger heads, wired. The lightest shades are almost beige.

White African everlastings—Twenty-eight pieces, most wired singly but some open flowers wired with buds.

Large white (cream) strawflowers—Fifteen, wired singly.

Miniature white strawflowers—Fourteen, wired singly.

White African daisies—Thirty-eight to forty daisies, wired into eighteen spikes of one full flower with one or two buds.

White (cream) amaranths—Forty to forty-four blossoms, wired into sixteen spikes of two or three flowers.

Large white floral buttons—Fifty-five buttons, wired into eleven spikes of five, each measuring two and one-half inches.

Miniature white floral buttons—Three hundred individual buttons wired into nineteen loose spikes, two and one-quarter inches long.

Maidenhair fern—Twenty-two pieces from the tips of the leaves, measuring three and one-half or four inches, wired.

Pampas grass—Seventeen four-inch spikes made by wiring three or four side shoots together.

===

Preparing the Container

The six inch bowl of the bird bath sits atop a pedestal, giving the container a height of three and one-half inches. Using a water-soluble glue, attach to the center of the bowl a square of Oasis that measures two and one-half inches. If you do not have time to allow the glue to dry thoroughly before beginning work on the arrangement, criss-cross some adhesive tape from the rim of the bowl and over the Oasis to the rim on the other side. The tape, or at least the ends of it, can be snipped off later.

The Assembly

Select the lightest pieces of golden cockscomb you can. Place the smallest one in the exact center of the Oasis so that its tip is nine and one-half inches from the table. Horizontally insert six pieces around the rim of the container, and allow them to extend one inch beyond it. Keep in mind that this is an all-around arrangement; you will have to keep turning the pedestal as you insert the plant materials. Next place six more pieces of celosia around the middle of the Oasis to complete the basic cone-like outline of the arrangement.

Insert one of the smaller white everlastings at the top of the arrangement and place the others among the clumps of cockscomb. Most of these will come out and up just as far as the cockscomb, although some of the buds may project out almost an inch farther.

The base of the bouquet has now been formed. All subsequent materials inserted will project out a little more.

Place two of the large, off-white strawflowers near the center top of the bouquet about as high as the cockscomb and the African everlastings. Horizontally insert eight around the rim of the bowl but projecting out beyond it by one to one and three-quarter inches. With five more blossoms, make an irregular row around the middle of the arrangement.

Now place the miniature white strawflowers. Start with three blossoms and put them in a circle around, but slightly below, the center top of the bouquet. Their tips will be about eight and one-half inches from the table top. Horizontally insert six around the rim of the container and finish with five in a more upright position and in an irregular row around the middle of the arrangement.

The yellow-centered white African daisies come out and up about two and one-half inches farther than the large strawflowers and are arranged in three irregular rows. Two go at the top of the arangement, nine are horizontally inserted near the rim of the bowl, and seven go around the broad middle of the bouquet. Be sure that you keep turning the container as you place the flowers.

Uneven spikes of white amaranths are also inserted in three irregular rows. Make one of four around the top. Insert seven in a not quite horizontal row above the rim of the bowl and place five around the middle.

The tips of the spikes of large white floral buttons come up and out beyond the large strawflowers by one and one-half to two inches. Place two spikes near the center top of the bouquet. Insert five at about forty degrees above the rim of the bowl and four in an even more upright position around the middle of the arrangement.

Spikes of miniature floral buttons come out as far as the spikes of large ones and are also arranged in three rows. Place three around the top of the bouquet, ten above the rim of the bowl, and six around the middle. Remember to keep turning the container.

The tips of maidenhair fern project out three inches farther than the large strawflowers. Three make a ring around the center top, ten are horizontally inserted at the rim of the bowl, and nine are zig-zagged around the broad middle of the arrangement.

Finally, place the spikes of grass with the tips of all but the top one out three and one-half inches farther than the large strawflowers. The spike at the center top is twelve and one-half inches from the table top. An irregular row of seven spikes is almost an inch above the rim of the bowl. Place three spikes around the tall center one, but a little lower than it is. Make a middle row of six spikes.

Blues and Whites in Wedgwood

This all-around bouquet is formal, pretty, and versatile. The blues of the hydrangea, statice, larkspur, and salvia perfectly pick up the blue of the Wedgwood vase, just as the white strawflowers, daisies, and buttons pick up the color of the container's decorative figures. The size and shape of the bouquet make it a handsome addition in innumerable settings, but any concentration of blues is likely to seem dull at night unless the spot is well lighted. For a yellow and white bouquet, use white larkspur and hydrangea with yellow statice and daisies. Either goldenrod or golden plume celosia might replace the spikes of blue salvia. For a pink and white arrangement, try pink larkspur and daisies with green or white hydrangea. German statice might then be used in place of salvia or goldenrod spikes.

The finished bouquet is a little over twelve inches high and is equally wide.

White African everlastings—Twenty, wired singly.

Large white (cream) strawflowers—Nine, wired singly.

Blue statice—Twenty-one spikes made of one or two natural clusters, wired.

White African daisies—Twenty-eight flowers or buds, wired in fourteen spikes of one bud or small flower over an open one.

Miniature white strawflowers—Seven, wired singly.

Blue hydrangea—Twenty-two clusters of blossoms, measuring two inches, broken from large heads, wired.

Miniature floral buttons—Fifteen uneven and loose spikes measuring two and one-half inches, each made of fourteen individual buttons, wired.

Blue larkspur—Sixteen pieces taken from the top four inches of natural spikes, wired.

Blue salvia—Twelve spikes made of two natural spikes, wired.

Preparing the Container

The blue and white Wedgwood vase is two and one-half inches high and three inches in diameter. Invert it on the top of a block of Oasis to make an impression of the opening and cut a circle through the three inch block. Push the Oasis into the vase far enough to leave one and one-half inches above the rim of the container.

The Assembly

Since this is an all-around arrangement, turn the vase as you insert all plant materials.

Place a white African everlasting in the center of the Oasis so that its tip is ten inches from the table. Horizontally insert ten of the larger flowers just above the rim of the vase and allow them to project out about two and one-quarter inches beyond it. Use nine of the flowers to fill in between the top flower and those at the rim, keeping in mind that you are constructing a loose cone shape.

The tip of the large white strawflower near the center of the Oasis is nine and one-half inches from the table. Five make an irregular row above the rim of the vase and three make a row between the flower at the top and the row at the bottom. These come out only a bit farther than the African everlastings.

Place four of the spikes of blue statice in a ten-inch high ring around the top center of the bouquet. Horizontally insert nine around the rim of the vase and make an irregular row of eight around the middle. The spikes in these rows come out one and one-half inches farther than the large white strawflowers.

Two of the white African daisies, which have yellow centers, are about nine and one-half inches from the table near the top center of the arrangement. Six make an irregular row just above the bottom row of large white strawflowers, and six are zig-zagged around the middle of the arrangement. All of these come out about one inch farther than the large strawflowers.

Place three of the miniature white strawflowers near the top of the bouquet. They should be one inch higher than the large strawflowers. Four go around the rim and project out two inches beyond the strawflowers.

Three of the clusters of blue hydrangea go around and are about even with the white African everlastings in the center top of the arrangement. Seven make an irregular row over the rim of the container and twelve are zig-zagged around the middle. The clusters in these rows come out one to two inches farther than the large white strawflowers.

The tip of the spike of miniature white buttons at the top of the bouquet is ten and one-half inches from the table. The row of eight above the rim of the container and the zig-zagged row of six around the middle come out one and one-half to two inches farther than the large white strawflowers.

If the top buds of the larkspur spikes are very small, break them off at a graceful point before measuring the four-inch pieces. Place three of the spikes around the top of the arrangement so their tips are about eleven inches from the table. Make an irregular row of seven near the bottom of the bouquet and one of six around the middle. Insert those near the bottom at about a twenty-five degree angle and those in the middle at about forty-five degrees. Both come out two and one-half to three inches beyond the large white strawflowers or approximately five inches from the container's rim.

The blue salvia spike in the top of the bouquet is twelve and one-half inches from the top of the table and is the highest flower of all. The row of six near the bottom and five around the middle of the bouquet come out two and one-half to three inches beyond the large strawflowers.

A Silver Bowl of Reds, Whites and Blues

The lovely all-around bouquet of red, white, and blue flowers, berries, and fern is the most popular arrangement made at Eighteenth Century Bouquet. It contains many different plant materials, a good number of which are wired into spikes that lighten and brighten the rather solid base of cockscomb and strawflowers. The spikes of tiny white starflowers and delicate white larkspur pick up the color of the African daisies which are the focal points of the arrangement.

Because of its size and shape, the bouquet is especially practical and versatile. It is low enough for a centerpiece, but is so simple and straightforward that it can be used in innumerable settings.

The basic design allows for the substitution of many other plant materials and colors. You could make a gold arrangement by using golden cockscomb and plume celosia, yellow statice and miniature straw-flowers, with white strawflowers. Yarrow could be used in place of the pepper berries, and immortelle might substitute for the salvia. For a mixed bouquet, use white strawflowers and blue, purple, white, or pink statice with yellow or red miniature strawflowers and white or blue lark-spur. A pink arrangement might include pink cockscomb, strawflowers, miniature strawflowers, statice, dock, and larkspur. Petticoat lace could replace the plume celosia. In any of these bouquets, amaranths could substitute for an unavailable flower, maidenhair fern could take the place of leather fern, and large or miniature floral buttons might be used instead of one of the spikes.

The finished arrangement is thirteen inches high and is equally wide.

Deep red cockscomb—Fifteen pieces, one inch to one and one-half inches in diameter, either small whole heads or pieces broken from larger heads, wired.

Large deep red strawflowers—Sixteen to eighteen, wired singly.

White African daisies—Forty-four blossoms, wired into twenty-two spikes of two each, a bud or small flower above a larger one.

Blue statice—Thirty-two small pieces broken from natural clusters and wired into sixteen spikes of two pieces.

Pink pepper berries—Thirty pieces broken from natural clusters, wired into fifteen graceful two-inch spikes, coated with clear floral spray.

Deep pink and red miniature strawflowers—Thirty-four blossoms, wired into seventeen spikes of two blossoms, a smaller one above a larger one.

Cinquefoil—Forty heads, wired into twenty spikes of two each.

White starflowers—One to two hundred tiny blossoms, wired into seventeen spikes of six to thirteen blossoms.

Red plume celosia—Thirty-six to fifty-four side shoots taken from the naturally heavy plumes, wired into eighteen delicate spikes of two or three shoots.

Green dock—Thirteen four-inch spikes made of side shoots, wired.

Blue salvia—Twenty to twenty-five natural spikes, wired into thirteen spikes of one or two pieces.

White larkspur—Seventeen natural spikes, wired singly.

Leather fern—Seventeen three-inch pieces taken from the tips of the leaves, wired.

Preparing the Container

The footed silver bowl is six inches in diameter and almost four inches high. Because it will need frequent polishing, use a papier mache or glass liner that can be removed easily. A paper liner, called a trump bowl and available from florists and hardwares, measures four inches in diameter and is two and one-half inches high. Make an imprint of the mouth of the liner on the top of a block of Oasis, and cut through the three-inch block along that line. Push the circle into the liner far enough for one inch of Oasis to be left above its rim. Place the filled liner in the silver bowl. If it seems to wobble a bit, stuff a little tissue paper between the liner and the bowl.

The Assembly

Since this is an all-around arrangement, you must turn the container as you insert the flowers. Try working on a lazy Susan, a plate, or some other smooth and round base. This is particularly important when the container has feet that might catch on the work surface.

Begin by placing the cockscomb, the fill that will give depth to the final bouquet. In the center of the Oasis put a piece of cockscomb whose tip is ten inches from the table. Next, horizontally insert seven of the largest and darkest pieces around the rim of the container, but extending two inches beyond it. They will look a bit like the spokes of a wheel. Now, fill in between the piece at the top and those at the rim by placing the cockscomb so as to create a cone-like shape. These must not bulge out beyond an imaginary line going from the top center piece to the tips of those at the rim. The pieces of cockscomb in the middle of the cone should be over the spaces between those at the rim.

Seven of the large, deep red strawflowers should be horizontally inserted among the cockscomb pieces at the rim of the container. Then, working up toward the top and keeping in mind that you are constructing a cone, place the strawflowers among the other pieces of cockscomb. You now have a reasonably solid base of cockscomb and strawflowers.

With the white African daisies, begin to bring the flowers out a bit farther. The tips of the spikes of daisies will come out about one-half inch beyond the strawflowers and cockscomb. Place one in the center of the Oasis and seven around the rim of the bowl. A few of those at the rim should be inserted at an angle so the flower head breaks the line of the top of the container. Zig-zag the rest of the daisies around the broad middle of the cone.

The spikes of blue statice come out even farther than the daisies and really break the solid conelike shape. The tips of the statice spikes jut out two inches farther than the cockscomb and strawflowers. Make a circle of four spikes around the center piece of cockscomb. Insert seven spikes around the rim of the bowl, some horizontally and some either inserted or bent so they, too, break the line of the bowl's rim. Zig-zag five around the broad middle of the bouquet. Remember to insert the flowers in more and more upright positions as you move from the rim to the top of the arrangement and to turn the bowl as you insert all plant materials.

The tips of the pink pepper berry spikes also come out two inches farther than the cockscomb. Although they are wired the way you wire spikes of flowers, they will naturally bend a bit and look more like sprays than spikes. Place three around the top, seven around the rim of the bowl, and five around the middle of the arrangement.

Insert a spike of miniature red strawflowers in the top center of the arrangement so that its tip is nine and one-half inches from the table. You may have to insert it in the top piece of cockscomb. The miniature strawflowers are now the highest point of the bouquet. Place nine spikes about two inches above the rim of the bowl and allow them to come out one and one-half inches farther than the cockscomb and large strawflowers. Zig-zag seven around the middle of the bouquet.

The spikes of moss-green cinquefoil come out one inch farther than the cockscomb. Three go around the top of the arrangement and six are just above the rim of the container. Use eleven spikes to fill in holes and hide wires around the middle of the bouquet. By now the cone-like shape has disappeared and the arrangement has begun to look looser and softer. The new materials introduced will be mostly in spike forms.

A spike of white starflowers at the very top is two and one-half to three inches higher than the cockscomb. Three more spikes go around, but a bit below it. The six spikes inserted at the bowl's rim and the seven around the middle come out two to two and one-half inches farther than the cockscomb.

The red plume celosia spike at the top is one-half inch lower than the top starflower spike. The celosia is too heavy to go above the delicate white starflowers, but it is important that the color be carried as far up the arrangement as possible. Insert three more celosia spikes around, but lower than, the center one. The rest of the plume celosia spikes come out two and one-half inches farther than the cockscomb. Place six around the rim and zig-zag eight around the middle.

At the peak of the arrangement is a spike of green dock whose tip is four inches higher than the cockscomb. The five dock spikes above the rim of the bowl and the seven around the bouquet's middle project three inches beyond the cockscomb. These are inserted in increasingly upright positions; none are horizontal.

Insert the blue salvia spikes in a pattern like that used for the dock, but allow it to project beyond the cockscomb by only three inches at the top and by about two and one-half inches in the rows.

Now add some brighter tones and lighter weights with spikes of white larkspur and pieces of leather fern. Three of the larkspur spikes go around the peak of the bouquet, but are lower than the green dock which remains the highest point in the arrangement. Insert nine at about a forty-five degree angle two inches above the bowl's rim. Place five around the middle in a slightly more upright position. The larkspur in the rows projects about five inches beyond the cockscomb.

The light and airy fern is added last. Insert three pieces around the top of the bouquet. Make an irregular row of seven at the rim of the container, allowing some of them to come down over it, and zig-zag seven around the middle. Both rows of fern project three and one-half inches beyond the cockscomb. Walk around the arrangement and insert small pieces of fern wherever you see a thin place.

Shades of Silver and Rose

Together, the white and gray plant materials and the shiny aluminum pâté mold create a silvery setting for the rose and lavender flowers. The arrangement is also an interesting study of contrasts in texture. There are stiff spikes of tiny white and papery German statice blossoms, soft clusters of small white pearly everlastings, strange little golf ball-like fruits of brunia, almost irridescent white African daisies, delicate silvery gray spikes of artemisia 'Silver King', and large, bold, and prickly globe thistles with a silvery blue cast. Mixed with these are the pink and rose tones of zinnias and miniature strawflowers, complemented by the lavender hues of domestic statice and loosestrife.

Although many of the characteristics of eighteenth century flower arranging can be found here, it is not a period piece. Somehow the plant materials and the container have a particular affinity for modern lucite, chrome, and glass. The arrangement is well suited for long surfaces and would be attractive on a dining table, a book case, or a room divider. It is twenty-four inches long, sixteen inches high, and fourteen inches deep at the container's rim.

German statice—Natural sprays or pieces broken from them, enough to loosely fill the container and provide a base for other plant materials, dampened for softness.

Pearly everlastings—Twenty-one clusters of the small white flowers, one and one-half to two inches in diameter, wired.

Rose and pink zinnias—Twenty-two blossoms, wired singly.

Brunia—Twenty-nine natural clusters of eight to twelve golf ball-like fruits, wired for height.

Lavender statice—Forty to forty-five small pieces or natural clusters, wired into twenty-one or twenty-three spikes.

Lavender loosestrife—Twenty-seven natural spikes of the small flowers, wired if necessary for height.

White African daisies—Nineteen open flowers, wired singly.

Rose colored miniature strawflowers—Twenty clusters of two or three wired.

Artemisia 'Silver King'—Ninety to one hundred tips of the natural spikes or of the side shoots, wired into thirty-one spikes of three or four pieces and measuring five or six inches.

Globe thistles—Eighteen thistles, wired singly.

Preparing the Container

The aluminum mold is fourteen inches long and a little over three inches high and wide. Trim one and one-half blocks of Oasis and wedge them into the mold. Then place another layer on top of that so the Oasis stands one and one-half inches above the rim of the mold. Secure the top layer to the bottom one with floral picks that are stuck through both layers. Trim off the exposed ends of the picks.

The Assembly

This is a back-to-back arrangement. Begin with a fan going from end to end along a middle line. Then complete the placement of each kind of plant material on one side, turn the container so the other long side is facing you, and repeat the pattern of all but the fan on that side. Check the ends of the bouquet before starting work with the plant material to be inserted next.

Use German statice to form the base for the arrangement. Put the statice in a plastic bag and sprinkle it with warm water. Seal the bag and allow it to stand for three or four hours. By then it will be soft and pliable enough to work with. Start by making a fan along the middle of the Oasis and going from one end of the container to the other. The center piece of statice is essentially ten inches high though a few of its spikes may be a little higher. The sprays at the ends of the mold are inserted horizontally and project beyond the ends of the mold by four or four and one-half inches. Now fill in between the center and the end pieces to create a fanlike shape. Horizontally insert a row just above the rim of the mold and allow them to come out about three inches. Fill in between the fan and the row at the rim, being careful that no bulge develops in the middle. Turn the container and repeat all but the fan on the other side. Check the ends of the arrangement to make sure that you have not neglected them and left thin places.

Make a fan of five clusters of white pearly everlastings. Put one in the center of the Oasis, one over each end of the container, and one not quite halfway down the fan between the center cluster and the ones on either end. Horizontally insert four clusters at the rim of the mold and bend two of them down to break the line of the container's edge. Make an irregular row of four clusters between the fan and the row at the rim. Repeat all but the fan on the other side. Check the ends and the profile before starting to place the zinnias.

To prepare the hollow-stemmed zinnias, put glue on the end of a wire and insert that into the zinnia stem about a half inch. If the hole in the stem is too large for the wire, put some tape on the wire before dipping it in glue and inserting it in the flower stem. Wrap tape around the stem at the base of the flower and onto the exposed wire. Place the zinnias near the clusters of pearly everlastings. Put six of the blossoms beside or just below the everlastings in the fan, but allow them to come out a bit farther than the white clusters do. Make a row of five above the rim of the mold and place three across the middle. Repeat the bottom and middle rows on the other side.

The clusters of brunia are to come out one and one-half to two inches farther than the everlastings. Seven of the clusters go in the fan, with the tip of the center one thirteen inches from the top of the table. Use four in an irregular row above the rim of the mold and zig-zag seven across the middle of the arrangement. Repeat the rows on the other side.

Start the seven-spike fan of lavender statice with a fifteen-inch-high spike in the middle. Place one over the rim of the container at either end and complete the fan by placing a spike to the left and the right of the center one, and then to the left and the right of those. Put four or five spikes in an irregular row at the rim of the mold and insert three across the middle. These should all come out as far as the brunia. Repeat the rows on the other side.

Use seven spikes of loosestrife to make a fan. Start with a center spike whose tip is fifteen inches from the top of the table. Insert spikes above the rim at the ends of the mold, and working with two additional pairs, complete the fan by first inserting a spike on the left and then one on the right of the center spike, and again one on the left and one on the right of those. The rows above the rim of the mold and across the middle of the arrangement are each made of five spikes that come out between three and one-half and four and one-half inches farther than the everlastings. Repeat the rows on the other side.

Use five of the smaller African daisies for the fan The tip of the center flower is eleven inches from the table. Horizontally insert three of the largest flowers above the rim of the mold and zig-zag four across the middle. Repeat the pattern for all but the fan on the other side.

Place four clusters of miniature rose strawflowers in the fan, but this time do not begin in the center. Two of the clusters are off center by two inches, one on the left and one on the right. Put one about half-way down the fan on either side. Make a row of three clusters over the rim of the mold and zig-zag five across the broad middle of the arrangement. Repeat all but the fan on the other side.

The spikes of artemisia do not come out quite so far as the loosestrife. There are nine in the fan, three over the rim of the mold, and eight in an irregular row across the middle. Turn the container and duplicate the rows on that side. Check the profile and the ends.

Place six globe thistles in the fan, starting on either side of the fan's center and working down to either end of the mold. The rows over the rim of the container and across the middle of the arrangement have three thistles apiece. Repeat the rows on the other side.

A Jug of Terra-Cottas and Greens

The clay jug of leaves, pods, grass, and flowers is informal and easy to assemble. Unlike the bouquets that consist of many varieties of plant materials, this all-around arrangement is a mass of green foliage and pods with a few flowers. The cockscomb and strawflowers pick up the color of the rather crude container, and the beige grain heads brighten the collection of somewhat muted tones.

A rustic or paneled den or library would make a perfect home for this large bouquet, through a traditional kitchen would also provide a harmonious setting. The arrangement is twenty-two inches high and is equally wide.

Beech leaves—Eighteen or more sprays of three glycerine-treated leaves, wired.

Rust and pale pink cockscomb—Twenty small natural heads or pieces broken from larger heads, one and one-half to two inches in diameter, wired.

Large pale pink strawflowers—Nine, wired singly.

Rust miniature strawflowers—Thirty blossoms, three wired singly and twenty-seven wired into nine spikes of three blossoms.

White (cream) amaranths—Fifty-six blossoms, wired into fourteen spikes of three to five blossoms.

Large rusty brown floral buttons—Twenty-four dyed buttons, wired into eight spikes of three each.

Pale green albizzia pods—Forty individual pods, wired into fifteen clusters of two to five pods.

Beige sea grass—Nineteen seed heads on natural stems.

Preparing the Container

The jug is six inches high and six inches wide at the base, but the opening is only about four inches in diameter. Invert the container on the top of the block of Oasis to make an impression of the opening. Cut through the three-inch block of Oasis at the indentation left by the jug's mouth and wedge it into the opening until only one inch is left above the rim.

The Assembly

Start the assembly with the sprays of beech leaves. Place one in the exact center of the Oasis so that its tip is seventeen inches from the table top. Horizontally insert seven sprays around the rim of the jug with some of the tips jutting over the rim by four inches and some of them hanging down over the container by four inches. Make a zig-zaged row of ten sprays between the row at the rim and the top spray. Fill in any holes with single leaves until you have a fairly solid ball of leaves. Remember that this is an all-around arrangement that must be turned as new material is added.

The clump of cockscomb in the middle of the Oasis should be almost fourteen inches from the table. Insert eight pieces around the rim of the jug, allowing them to jut over it by three inches. Bend some of these down so they break the line of the container's top. Push four more clumps of cockscomb well into the middle of the arrangement to help hide wires of the leaves. Then zig-zag five more clumps around that middle. Do not push these in so far, but be careful that they do not create a bulge. Finally, place two more pieces near, but slightly below, the one at the top.

Three pale pink strawflowers go among the pieces of cockscomb at the top of the arrangement. Place three more among the pieces of cockscomb at the container's rim, and three around the middle. All of these come up and out just as far as the cockscomb.

Put three single rust strawflowers around the top of the arrangement so their tips are about fourteen inches from the table. Five spikes of blossoms go around the container's rim and four are inserted around the middle of the bouquet.

Place a spike of white amaranths in the center of the arrangement, with its tip sixteen inches from the table. Put five spikes among the cockscomb and pink strawflowers at the rim of the jug and zig-zag eight around the broad middle of the bouquet.

The top center spike of rusty brown floral buttons is fifteen and one-half inches from the table. The tips of the three spikes that project up and out from the bottom of the arrangement are four and one-half inches beyond the container's rim. Four spikes go around the middle.

The spray of five albizzia pods in the center of the bouquet is eighteen inches high. Place five pod sprays about one inch above the container's rim so that they jut out beyond the rim by almost seven inches. Put four sprays around, but slightly below, the one at top center. Zig-zag five around the broad middle of the arrangement.

Finally, place the long seed heads. Put one in the center of the arrangement so that its tip is twenty-two inches from the table top. Horizontally insert eight around the jug's rim and allow them to extend seven or eight inches beyond it. Place five around, but lower than, the central seed head and zig-zag five around the middle. These should come out five or six inches farther than the celosia.

Classic Simplicity

These arrangements contain fewer varieties of flowers and less contrast in texture than do the traditional or harmonious bouquets and they display less contrast in color than the traditional ones. For the most part, one or sometimes two kinds of flowers play the major role and the other plant materials are there to provide a background for them or to complement either the flowers or the container.

The compositions of money and baby's breath and of Queen Anne's lace and leaves are the epitome of simplicity. The peonies in the delft bowl are accompanied primarily by leaves, but the yellow statice picks up the color of the flower centers. In both the dogwood arrangements, one in a pewter pitcher and another in a china bowl, all the other plant materials pick up either the white of the petals or the green of the blossoms' centers. The bold and dramatic orange lily-like flowers made of Chinese lanterns have been given a backdrop of laurel leaves and a spikey accent of tiny pods.

Although most colonial flower arrangers seem to have had a distinct preference for the large "printy" arrangements containing many varieties of flower materials in contrasting colors, the reports of European plant finders describe glasses full of amaranths and pearly everlastings. They suggest that during the summer the fireplaces were decorated with boughpots filled with large branches of fruit blossoms from the forest and masses of wild flowers, no doubt including goldenrod, from the field. An arrangement much like that of Chinese lanterns might very well have hidden an empty fireplace in an eighteenth century home. Roses, which the English loved so much, must have been the primary ingredient in arrangements of all sizes and shapes.

The containers of the classic arrangements are neither so formal as those used for the traditional bouquets nor as informal as some of those holding the harmonious compositions.

Ingredients used in the following arrangements are listed in the order of their use.

Roses in a Pewter Bowl

See color pages for illustration.

The all-around arrangement of red roses, blue delphinium, and white hydrangea with greens looks much like a fresh bouquet. Although the design is quite simple, the roses give it a feeling of elegance and make it suitable for formal settings and occasions. Lacey fern and hydrangea add a lightness and airiness and provide an interesting contrast in texture, while the delphinium contributes a spikey accent. The bouquet is low enough for a dining table and just the right size for coffee and end tables.

Red roses—Sixteen blossoms and buds, dried in silica gel with one inch or one and one-half inch stems.
Pussy willow stems—Fifty-six, dried in gel.
Boxwood—Thirty pieces that are seven inches long and five and one-half inches wide, dried in gel, not wired.
Rose leaves—Sixteen three-leaf sprays with one-inch stems, dried in gel.
Blue delphinium—Ten spikes of three to five flowers taken from the tips of the natural spikes and twelve large side blossoms, the spikes wired, the side blossoms given false stems.
Maidenhair fern—Twenty-six pieces from five to six inches long.
White hydrangea—Eighteen pieces, wired into clusters measuring one and one-half to two and one-half inches.

Preparing the Container

To make cleaning and polishing the six-inch by four-inch pewter bowl easier, use either a glass or papier mache liner. Invert the liner on a block of Oasis to get an outline of its opening and cut a piece big enough to fill the liner and project one inch above it. Push the Oasis into the liner and secure the liner to the bowl with floral clay.

The Assembly

Because this is a rather open bouquet in which wires of at least the tall flowers would be visible, make false stems for the red roses in the upper part of the bouquet. Pussy willow stems are ideal for this because they are woody, have soft centers into which it is easy to poke wires, and do not have thorns. If the stem seems too brown, color it with green spray. Put some glue on the end of a wire and shove it into a pussy willow stem as far as you can, at least half an inch. Cut off all but one inch of the exposed wire, enough to push into the rose stem. Put a drop of glue on the end of the wire and push it into the rose stem until it and the pussy willow stem meet. See page 20.

Place the smallest rose bud in the exact center of the Oasis with its tip eleven and one-half inches from the table. Put four small roses or larger buds around but just below it. Next, insert the six largest roses in an irregular and not quite horizontal row above the rim of the bowl. Zig-zag five roses around the broad middle of the bouquet. Remember to turn the container as you insert all plant materials.

Use sprays of boxwood to hide the Oasis and to fill the space between the liner and the bowl. Some of these should be inserted horizontally and allowed to protrude three to four inches beyond the rim of the bowl. Others are slightly more upright. The tips of the eight or ten still more upright sprays inserted in the middle of the Oasis are about ten inches from the table.

Place the sprays of rose leaves near the roses so it looks as though they are on the same stems. The smaller sprays that go near the top of the arrangement, where their "stems" might be exposed, are given false stems in the same way the roses were. The leaves extend out beyond the roses by two or three inches.

To prepare the blue delphinium, make a hole in a pussy willow stem, put a drop of glue on the short delphinium stem, and insert that in the hole of the pussy willow stem. The delphinium stems are too fragile to be treated the way the rose stems were.

Put two delphinium spikes near the single rose bud at the top of the bouquet. Make an irregular row of twelve large single flowers above the rim of the container and zig-zag eight spikes around the broad middle of the bouquet. The tips of the spikes project beyond the roses by one inch or one and one-half inches.

Place three pieces of fern around the rose bud at the top and allow them to come out four inches beyond the rose. Make an irregular row of ten pieces at the rim of the bowl and extending five inches beyond it. Some of these will droop over the side of the bowl. Hold the arrangement up at eye level or a little higher to make sure that none of the structure is visible. Use eight pieces of fern to fill in thin places and make an irregular row slightly above the fern at the rim. Place five around but a little lower than the top sprays of rose leaves.

Most of the clusters of hydrangea are used to fill in holes and hide any still exposed Oasis in the bottom half of the bouquet. These should be even with the roses or project beyond them by just a bit. Finally, place a few hydrangea clusters in the top half of the arrangement. These should be pushed in a little farther than the roses.

Chinese Lanterns in a Woven Basket

Brilliant orange Chinese lanterns that have been turned into tiger lily-like flowers make a bold and dramatic display when combined with the coppery green of glycerine-treated laurel leaves. The dark brown of the wide-ribbed basket provides a perfect contrast in both color and texture. Although the arrangement is rather stylized, it has great versatility and would be a handsome addition to almost any decor. It could liven and brighten a dark corner in a contemporary house or grace a large piano in a room with traditional furniture.

The finished half-bouquet is twenty-nine inches high, twenty-eight inches wide, and fifteen inches deep at the rim of the basket.

Laurel leaves—Thirteen clusters of glycerine-treated leaves with up to seventeen leaves on a stem, wired, especially if they are to hang over the rim.

Chinese lanterns—Fourteen branches of lanterns, wired if necessary for manipulation.

Hairy beard-tongue—Thirteen stems of small seed pods, wired for height.

===

Preparing the Container

The basket shown in the photograph is Japanese and is made of sea weed, but many commercially available baskets could be used. Just be sure that it is made of wide ribs and is a good rich brown. A straw-colored one could be dyed.

The basket is nine inches high and has a six-inch opening. Its liner is seven inches high and has a three-inch opening.

Invert the liner on the top of a block of Oasis to make an impression of the opening and cut a piece that size through the three-inch-thick block. Wedge the Oasis into the top two inches of the liner, allowing a one-inch collar to stand above the rim of the liner. Now put the liner in the center of the basket and stuff enough crumpled newspaper between the liner and the basket to make the liner quite steady.

The Assembly

The assembly begins with the placement of the clusters of laurel leaves. First make a fan of leaves across the back of the Oasis. Put a branch just to the right of the center so that its tip is twenty-six inches from the table top. The tip of the branch to the left of that is twenty-one inches from the table, and the one to the right of the twenty-six-inch branch stands nineteen inches high. The tips of the leaves in the exact center of the Oasis are twenty-three inches from the table. To the left of that middle branch, place another whose tip is twenty inches above the table. The branch of leaves to the right of the middle one is nineteen inches high. See the solid lines in the drawing.

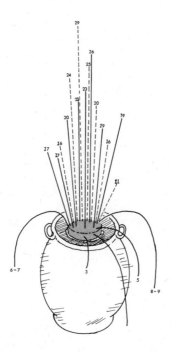

Now begin working toward the front of the Oasis and around the rim of the container. Put one branch just back of the handle on the right. It should hang down over the rim of the basket by eight or nine inches. The one back of the handle on the left hangs down only six or seven inches. The leaves in the middle of the front of the basket are inserted horizontally so they just clear the rim of the basket and project beyond it by three inches. To the right of the branch in the center front, insert one so that its tip barely clears the table top. To the left of the center-front leaf spray, place a branch that stands seventeen inches from the table. Finally, place leaf sprays just in front of the handle on either side of the basket. The one on the right hangs down over the rim of the basket by five inches and the one on the left stands up seventeen inches.

Now it is time to transform the lanterns into flowers. If they are very dry, quickly pass them under warm running water. Then, because the pods or lanterns are very fragile, it is a good idea to put just a drop of Duco cement on the base of the pod where it is joined by the stem.

Look closely at the lanterns and you will see that they have four major and four minor veins. To turn the closed pods into flowers, start at the pointed end and, with a small pair of scissors, cut from the tip toward the base on the major, or the minor, or both veins. The farther you cut toward the base of the pod, the more open the flower will be. Remembering the general rule—that buds and smaller flowers belong at the top of an arrangement and the fuller and heavier ones in the lower part—prepare the branches of lanterns. Turn the petals of the full flowers back with your fingers.

If a pod should fall off while you are working, simply take another one from an extra branch or from a less conspicuous place on one of the stems you are using, punch a hole in the pod near, but not at, the place where the stem had been attached, put Duco cement in the hole, and insert the new flower on the stem that has lost its blossom. Allow the cement to dry thoroughly before touching the pod again. Chinese lanterns, which naturally have reasonably long stems, need not be wired, but they can be if you want a particular bend or curve.

Construct a fan of lanterns in front of the leaves across the back of the Oasis. The tip of the center one is twenty-nine inches from the table. To the left of that, the first should be twenty-four inches high and a second one on the left, sixteen inches high. To the right of the tallest stem of lanterns are four whose tips are twenty-five, twenty, sixteen, and eleven inches from the table. The tip of the branch in front center is ten inches from the rim of the basket and thirteen inches from the table. To its right, a branch juts out six inches and bends down to within six inches of the table. The one on the left of front center is seven inches from the rim and the table. Use the remaining branches to fill in between the lanterns in the back fan and those that are at the front rim of the basket. Lightly coat the lanterns with clear floral spray. This must be done after they are in position in the arrangement. See the broken lines in the drawing.

Finally, place the pods of beard-tongue. They should not come out and up so far as the lanterns. Four go among the laurel leaves in the back fan; four make an irregular row that is almost horizontal to the table just above the rim of the basket, and five are zig-zagged across the middle of the arrangement.

Now walk away from the arrangement and look at it from several angles. Hide any exposed Oasis with additional sprays of laurel leaves.

Oriental Chives in Glass

Clusters of tiny, white, starlike flowers of Oriental chive, graceful maidenhair fern, and spikes of golden freesia make a particularly delicate bouquet with an especially fresh look and feel. The small, all-around arrangement lends itself to glass. It would be attractive in many settings —but especially on a small table or desk in a powder room or bedroom. It is ten inches high and eight inches wide.

Oriental chive blossoms—Twenty-nine or thirty natural clusters with one-half-inch stems.

Chive stems—Thirty-five chive stems, dried separately.

Yellow freesia—Nine spikes of flowers and buds with their natural stems.

Maidenhair fern—Twenty-four four-inch pieces of fern broken from the tips of the leaves, wired, and a few pieces from which the leaflets have been removed.

Queen Anne's lace stems—A number of dried stems in a variety of thicknesses.

Preparing the Container

The roly-poly glass measures two inches at the base, three inches at its widest point, and three inches at the opening. Invert the glass on the top of a block of Oasis and make an impression of the opening. Cut a circle slightly larger than that impression through the block of Oasis, then cut one inch off the bottom of the circle so it is two inches thick. One inch of the circle is to be inserted in the glass and the other inch is to rise above its rim. Cut three-quarters of one inch from the outer edge of the Oasis and level with the glass, leaving a column that is one-inch high and one and one-half inches in diameter. Insert the Oasis in

the glass, but do not wedge it in firmly yet. If it seems to wobble, insert wooden floral picks that have been dipped in glue into the raised center just at the rim of the glass. Trim off the end of the picks, leaving only enough to keep the Oasis steady as you insert the flowers.

The Assembly

Prepare the clusters of Oriental chive blossoms by giving them longer stems. To do that simply put a drop of Duco cement on the tip of the stem attached to the cluster and insert it in one of the chive stems that was dried separately. Place a flower cluster in the center of the raised Oasis so its tip is between nine and ten inches from the table. Horizontally insert into the side of the raised circle seven flower clusters. Allow them to jut out over the container's rim from one to two inches. Place four more clusters around, but one inch lower than, the center cluster. Use the rest of the chive blossoms to make two irregular circles of clusters around the Oasis between the five clusters at the top and those at the rim. Remember to turn the glass as you insert the flowers and place them in more and more upright positions as you move from the bottom to the top of the arrangement.

Select the spikes of yellow freesia with the most buds and the smallest flowers for the top of the bouquet. If their natural stems are not long enough, add a piece of Queen Anne's lace stem. Use a pin or a wire to make a hole in the end of the stem to be added. Put a drop of Duco cement on the freesia stem and insert it into the hole. If you need to bend the stem of any of the freesia spikes, insert the end of a piece of wire in a Queen Anne's lace stem. Lay the other end along the freesia stem, with about one-quarter inch of wire between the two stems. Tape the wire and the freesia stem together and carry the tape down over the wire and barely onto the added stem. See page 19.

One freesia spike goes into the top center of the arrangement with its tip nine and one-half inches from the table. Horizontally insert four spikes around the rim of the glass and allow them to project two inches beyond it. Make a circle of four more spikes half way up the arrangement. These must be in a more upright position and their tips should be two and one-half inches beyond the container's rim.

The maidenhair fern is used to fill in holes in the arrangement and particularly to hide its structure. Start filling in at the top of the bouquet, but do not allow any of the fern to be higher than the top center cluster of chive flowers. Reserve the fern pieces with natural bends for use around the rim of the glass. Hold the container at eye level, or even a little higher, as you insert the fern in the lower part of the arrangement. Be careful that none of the Oasis, either in or above the glass, is left exposed.

Now remove the bouquet and the Oasis from the glass and shake out any little pieces of Oasis that may have fallen into the glass while you were working. Wash and polish the glass.

To make a dried flower arrangement in a glass container seem realistic, some stems must be visible. Insert in the *bottom* of the Oasis a few of the black maidenhair stems from which the leaflets have been removed and some chive and Queen Anne's lace stems. All of these should be of varying lenths and inserted at different angles. Do not try to insert a stem for each flower in the arrangement; just make a suggestion. Fifteen or twenty stems should be enough.

Very carefully put a little Duco cement around the top of that part of the Oasis that fits into the glass and return the bouquet to the container. Wedge it in securely, but be careful that no more pieces of Oasis fall into the glass. The floral picks will hold the arrangement in place until the glue has dried. Remove them then.

Money and Baby's Breath in a Glass Compote

There is an elegant simplicity in this arrangement of just baby's breath and money. The silvery white of the plant materials catches and reflects natural and artificial light, giving the bouquet a sparkly effect. It would be especially appropriate as a wedding decoration and would add light and life in a setting of Christmas greens. The nineteen-inch by fifteen-inch arrangement is probably too delicate for a paneled room or one with heavy furniture, but it would be ideal in a modern glass and chrome setting or in a more traditional French provincial environment.

Both baby's breath and money are easily grown and are hang dried. Neither need to be wired.

Baby's Breath—Enough sprays of various sizes to create the basic shape desired.

Money—Seventeen side shoots with several coins.

Preparing the Container

The glass compote, which is etched with gold, is nine inches high. The bowl on top of the pedestal is eight inches in diameter and two and one-half inches deep. Since the Oasis must not show through this very light and airy arrangement, prepare a small white container that can be set in the compote. The top of an aerosol can, a small cup, or any other white container that is about two inches high and two and one-half inches in diameter will do. Make an imprint of the top of the container on the top of a block of Oasis and cut a piece that will be one-half inch higher than the cup. Push the Oasis into the cup and secure the cup to the compote with floral clay.

The Assembly

Dampen the baby's breath a bit and place it in a plastic bag for a few hours before you are ready to begin the assembly. In the center of the Oasis insert a spray whose tip will be nineteen inches from the table. Horizontally insert sprays around the rim of the compote and allow them to project beyond its rim by three and one-half to four inches and to hang over the edge anywhere between one-half to four inches. Now fill in between the top and bottom, changing the lengths of the sprays and their angle of insertion to produce a bouquet shaped like half an oval. Since baby's breath is so webby, the last pieces of baby's breath can be inserted into the thick tangle without going into the Oasis. Put a little glue on the stems and push them into the arrangement wherever there seem to be holes. They will find something to stick to.

In the center of the Oasis, insert a piece of money whose tip will be one-half to one inch taller than the tallest spray of baby's breath. Around the rim of the compote, insert nine side branches of coins so they come out one inch beyond the baby's breath. Every other one of these should be horizontal to the work table and the others should be more upright. Arrange seven side shoots in an irregular row around the broad middle of the arrangement, allowing them to come out one inch or one and one-half inches farther than the baby's breath but retaining the shape formed by it.

A China Bowl of Greens and Whites

White dogwood blossoms with green centers are the focal points of this rather formal but fresh looking bouquet. The white bowl and all of the other plant materials complement these flowers by picking up their colors and providing a delicate background for their display. The arrangement, which can be viewed from any direction, would be attractive in a period or contemporary setting so long as the furniture is not too heavy. It might go on a wood or glass coffee table or could be used as a centerpiece in a small but formal dining room.

This arrangement could also be made with either marigolds or zinnias as substitutes for the dogwood.

The oval bouquet is fifteen inches long, a little over twelve inches high, and twelve inches deep if measured from spike tip to spike tip at the container's rim.

Beech leaves—Fifteen sprays of three leaves, glycerine-treated, wired or on natural stems.

Dogwood blossoms—Twenty-four flowers on Queen Anne's lace stems.

Queen Anne's lace stems—Twenty-four stems of varying lengths and thicknesses.

Maidenhair fern—Twenty-three four to six-inch pieces of fern taken from the tips of the leaves, leaflets removed from the bottom inch of stem, wired.

White larkspur—Twenty natural spikes, wired only if the stems are not straight and firm.

Large floral buttons—One hundred and fifteen floral buttons, dyed a light green, wired into twenty-three spikes of five butts.

Preparing the Container

The china bowl, really a sauceboat, is five and one-half inches long and four inches high. Because of the sloping sides of the bowl, cutting a piece of Oasis to fit it would be difficult. Instead, use a liner. The cap of an aerosol spray can or any other container about two inches high and wide will work well. Invert the liner on the top of a block of Oasis to make an impression of its opening. Cut through the three-inch-thick block. Push the piece of Oasis into the liner until only about one and one-half inches is left above the rim. Secure the liner to the bowl of the sauceboat with floral clay.

The Assembly

Since the bouquet is in the shape of a long oval, the techniques used for back-to-back arrangements are applicable here. Except for the plant material in the fan, place all of one kind of flower on one side of the arrangement, then turn the container and repeat the pattern on the other side. The secret of success in this method is remembering to check the ends frequently. They will be thin if they are neglected.

Begin the assembly by placing the beech leaves, using the natural stems unless they are too short. Put one spray in the middle of the Oasis with its tip ten and one-half inches from the table. Insert a spray that droops a bit just above the container's rim at either end. These should jut out about five inches beyond the bowl's edge. Now insert two leaf sprays between the one at the top and those at the ends of the sauceboat to make a fan. Insert three sprays at the rim of the bowl between those at either end, allowing them to come out three and one-half inches from the rim. Now insert two leaf sprays between the one at the top and the row at the rim. Turn the container and repeat the middle row of two sprays and the one of three at the rim.

Before preparing the almost stemless dogwood blossoms, hold them against the arrangement of leaves to be sure that you know where you want them. They are very delicate and must be handled as little as possible. The flowers, which are the focal points of the bouquet, need false stems because they cannot be pushed into the rather loose arrangement far enough to hide wires. Make a hole in the end of a Queen Anne's lace stem by pushing a pin or wire into its center. Put a drop of glue on the end of the flower's stem and insert it into the hole of the stem to be added. You can use tweezers for this operation or actually hold the center of the blossom since it is quite firm.

Place a dogwood blossom on either side of, but about two or two and one-half inches below the tallest leaf. Insert one of the largest blossoms just over the rim of the bowl at either end of the arrangement. They should project three or three and one-half inches beyond it. Make an irregular row of four flowers at the rim of the bowl between those that go over the ends. Allow these to come out over the bowl by a little more than two inches. Zig-zag five blossoms across the middle of the bouquet, between the top flowers and the row at the rim. Turn the container around and repeat the pattern on the other side.

Select a six-inch piece of maidenhair fern for the center top of the bouquet. Its tip is eleven and one-half inches from the table top. Put another six-inch piece over the rim of the bowl at either end of the arrangement. Place three pieces of fern at the rim of the bowl and between those at either end. These too should droop over the bowl, some almost touching the table top. Now select the shorter pieces of fern. Three of these make a row below the top center piece of maidenhair and protrude beyond the dogwood by three and one-half or four inches. With four more short pieces of fern, make an irregular row between the row of three and the row at the container's rim. Turn the container and repeat the rows on the other side.

The spikes of white larkspur are about the same length as the fern pieces, but they are more erect. Make a circle of four flower spikes around the spray of beech leaves at the top of the arrangement, but not quite so high as the tallest piece of fern. At either end of the arrangement and just above the rim of the bowl, place a larkspur spike that will jut over the edge by three and one-half or four inches. Still working just over the rim of the container, place three spikes between those at the ends, but allow these to jut out only a little more than two inches. Then make a middle row of four spikes, being careful to place one near either end of the arrangement. Turn the container, and repeat the pattern for all but the top circle of flowers and those at the ends on the other side.

Finally, place the spikes of floral buttons. One spike, whose tip is ten inches from the table, goes at the center top of the arrangement. A spike that projects four inches beyond the bowl's rim goes at either end. Make a row of three spikes just above the rim of the container and between those at either end, but allow these to come out only one inch farther than the dogwood blossoms. Make a zig-zagged row of seven spikes half way up the bouquet. Repeat all but the spikes at center top and at the ends of the boat.

Now step back and walk around the arrangement. Deeply insert small pieces of fern wherever there are holes or thin spots.

Queen Anne's Lace on an Antiqued Copper Charger

A beautiful and much underestimated weed is here transformed into a large, yet delicate, arrangement that will become the focal point of almost any room. It picks up the sunlight from a window, but looks quite white if placed where it can catch the light from a lamp. A dark wall or backdrop becomes much lighter and brighter in its presence.

The completed bouquet is fifteen inches high and seventeen inches wide at the base.

Laurel-leaf sprays—Eighteen to twenty sprays of glycerine-treated leaves, taken from the tips of the branches, measuring from eight to eleven inches, and bearing from three to twenty leaves.

Spirea-leaf branches—Twelve branches of glycerine-treated leaves, measuring up to twelve inches.

Queen Anne's lace blossoms—Thirty-two heads of buds and flowers, dried with as long stems as possible.

Queen Anne's lace stems—Additional gel-dried stems to lengthen stems dried with blossoms.

Preparing the Container

The fifteen-inch plate has quite a deep flare from a flat base that is nine inches in diameter, but even that flare is not deep enough to hide a liner big enough to hold the arrangement. To solve that problem, cut a five-inch circle of cardboard and glue on it a circle of Oasis that is three inches high and three inches in diameter. Affix the cardboard and Oasis to the plate with floral clay. The cardboard is used to protect the plate from insoluble glue.

The Assembly

Start this all-around arrangement by placing a twenty-leaf spray of laurel leaves in the center of the Oasis so that its tip is eleven inches from the table. Then horizontally insert four eight-inch sprays with eight or nine leaves at the rim of the charger, but extending out about one inch beyond the edge. Between these, but a little higher on the Oasis, insert four five-inch sprays with about six leaves so that their tips come out over the flat bottom, but not over the flare, of the plate.

With the branches of spirea leaves, begin the outline of the cone-like shape of the arrangement. In the center of the Oasis place a branch whose tip is sixteen inches from the table. Near the bottom of the Oasis, make a circle of five branches of leaves whose tips are five inches from the table and project out as far as the rim of the charger. A circle of six branches goes between the lower row of spirea leaves and the tip of the tallest branch. By now the Oasis should be pretty well covered. If it isn't, push a few short sprays of laurel leaves in close to it.

Most of the Queen Anne's lace blossom will need longer stems than could be dried with them. In those cases, make a pin hole in a stem that is thicker than the one on the flower. Put a drop of glue on the flower stem and insert that in the pin hole of the stem to be added. Use three buds or small flowers to make a small circle around the laurel and spirea leaves. That circle should be fifteen inches from the table. Horizontally insert eleven or twelve of the larger flower heads in the Oasis so that some of the flowers rest on the rim of the plate and others are just a bit above it. With fourteen additional flower heads fill in the middle of the arrangement to complete the cone outline. Finally, break that outline with a few smaller flowers that come out about one inch farther than the others in the lower two-thirds of the arrangement.

Peonies in a Delft Bowl

See color pages for illustration.

The massive and formal arrangement of pink and white peonies, leather fern, and yellow statice might have graced a heavy chest or table in one of the manor houses of eighteenth century Virginia, for the gardeners and householders of that period imported both peonies and delft ware. An impressive Dutch delft punch bowl is able to carry the large and dense blossoms well, but the flowers are too forceful for a traditional bouquet of many plant materials. Here they are allowed to speak for themselves. Spikes of statice pick up the yellow centers of the peonies, and the fern gives the arrangement a lighter and looser feeling.

A yellow and blue creation might be made with the same design, using large yellow marigolds and statice to match the blue of the bowl. Orange marigolds and yellow statice would also make a handsome bouquet.

This all-around arrangement needs a lot of space since it is twenty-two inches high and is equally wide.

Leather fern—Nine whole leaves, ten nine-inch pieces taken from the tips of the leaves, and from nine to eleven sprays of leaflets taken from the sides of the leaves, all pressed, wired, and coated with moss-green floral spray.

Pink and white peony blossoms and buds—Ten large pink peonies, seven medium white blossoms, nine or ten medium pink peonies, two pink buds, and four white buds, all dried in silica gel with one inch or one and one-half inch stems.

Pussy willow stems—Thirty-three gel-dried stems for false peony stems.

Peony leaves—Twenty-two natural sprays of leaves taken from the tips of the branches, wired and taped, the tape coated with green florist spray and the leaves with clear spray.

Yellow statice—Eighty to one hundred natural clusters, wired into thirty-six spikes of two or three clusters.

Preparing the Container

A liner of some kind is necessary to avoid gluing the Oasis to the bottom of the bowl. A papier mache one that is six inches in diameter and three inches high will do very well, but a mixing bowl about that size can also be used. Cut a square of Oasis as large as the width of the block will allow and push it into the liner on which you have spread some glue. Do not be alarmed if the corners of the Oasis crumble. Now it is level with the rim of the liner. Place a second piece of Oasis, this one only one and one-half inches high, on top of the first and secure it by inserting wooden floral picks through both pieces. Trim off the exposed ends of the picks and attach the liner to the bowl with floral clay.

The Assembly

Since this is an all-around arrangement, remember to keep turning the container as you insert the plant materials.

Place two leather fern leaves just off the center of the Oasis so their tips are between seventeen and eighteen inches from the top of the table. Horizontally insert four leaves around the rim of the container with their tips seven inches beyond the rim. Three leaves go around the middle of the Oasis and are angled out to establish the basic outline of the arrangement. Use the nine-inch pieces of fern to fill in that outline. Place them between the rows of whole fern leaves.

To prepare the peonies, insert one inch of the end of a two and one half-inch wire into the peony stem or lay the end of the wire along the stem. Starting at the base of the flower, wrap floral tape around the stem, or the stem and the wire, leaving one and one-half inches of exposed wire. Tear off the tape. Push the exposed end of wire into a pussy willow stem, leaving one-quarter inch of wire between the two stems. Starting at the base of the flower again, wrap tape over the first tape and continue taping over the exposed wire and down over one inch of the pussy willow stem. The wire between the two stems makes a kind of elbow which you can bend to control the direction of the flower faces. See page 21.

Put a peony bud in the center of the Oasis with its tip eighteen inches from the top of the table. Arrange the other buds around but slightly below it. Horizontally insert five of the largest peonies around the rim of the bowl, but projecting four inches beyond it. Place five more of the large blossoms almost half way up the arrangement and over the spaces between the peonies at the rim. Next intersperse the medium peonies among the others, being careful to keep the pinks and whites separated. All of these flowers should be pushed in one to four inches farther than the fern.

Now step back and look at the arrangement from all angles. Use the sprays of fern leaflets to fill in any holes and especially to make sure that none of the Oasis is visible. These pieces of fern should be pushed in quite far.

Place a spray of peony leaves in the center of the bouquet with its tip twenty-one inches from the table. Make an irregular row of leaves over the rim of the bowl and projecting out beyond the peonies by four or five inches. Zig-zag the rest of the sprays around the broad middle of the arrangement with their tips three to four inches beyond the peonies. Be sure that the leaves do not block the view of the flowers.

The longest spike of statice goes in the center of the bouquet and is twenty-two inches high. At the rim of the container, make an irregular row of horizontally inserted statice spikes that come out three or four inches farther than the peonies. Use the rest of the statice spikes to make two irregular rows between the one at the top and those over the bowl's rim.

Dogwood in a Pewter Pitcher

The white dogwood blossoms and the intriguing, off-white or gray, golfball-like fruits of brunia are the focal points of this arrangement, but the star-like shapes of the fully opened green pods of gas plant are also fascinating. The laurel leaves seem to pick up some of the luster of the old pewter flagon. In earlier days the flagon would probably have been used for syrup, but when you think of it as a flower container it seems to call for sturdy plant materials. That is what makes brunia so appropriate here. Although arrangers of dried flowers often try to hide stems and wires, the coarse and rope-like brunia stems add an unusual and pleasant contrast in texture.

This tall, all-around arrangement would be ideal for a small entrance hall, on a narrow table, or on a mantle, especially one of the very narrow ones found in so many eighteenth century houses.

The bouquet is thirteen inches high and nine inches wide.

Brunia fruits—Twenty natural sprays with seven or eight fruits, wired if necessary for height.

Laurel leaves—Thirty glycerine-treated leaves, wired singly or in clusters.

Light green gas plant seed pods—Thirty-nine seed pods, pulled off stems, wired into thirteen spikes of three pods.

Dogwood blossoms—Twelve blossoms with the longest possible stems and wired.

'Navajo zinnias'—Fifteen, wired singly.

===

Preparing the Container

The pitcher is six and one-half inches high, not including the lid which will be propped back for the arrangement. It is three inches wide at the bulge, but the opening is a bit smaller than that.

Cut a three-inch-high circle of Oasis just large enough for a snug fit in the neck of the pitcher and push it in until only one and one-half inches is left exposed. The lid of the container is automatically held back by the column of Oasis rising above the rim of the pitcher.

The Assembly

Treat this arrangement as you would an all-around one even though the lid can be seen from one side.

Select the largest spike of brunia for the center and place it so that its tip is thirteen inches from the table. Horizontally insert nine sprays of varying sizes just over the rim of the pitcher, allowing them to jut beyond it by two and one-half inches. Use seven sprays to make an irregular row around the middle of the bouquet. Now hold the arrange-ment at eye level or above and push the last three pieces of brunia into the Oasis wherever it seems most exposed.

Put a four-leaf spray of laurel leaves into the center of the Oasis so that its tip is one-half inch above the top spray of brunia fruits. Insert a six-leaf spray in front of, but a little lower than, the first one. At the rim of the pitcher, horizontally insert three sprays of three to five leaves and allow them to droop over the side of the container. Be sure these are evenly distributed around the rim. Make a middle row of five single leaves. Insert them at about a forty-five degree angle and allow them to come out one inch farther than the brunia.

Put a spike of gas plant pods on either side of the top spike of brunia with their tips one and one-half inches below the tips of the top spray of laurel leaves. Use five spikes in an irregular row just above the rim of the pitcher and push them in a little farther than the brunia. Another irregular row, this one of six spikes, goes around the middle of the arrangement. Remember to turn the container as you insert the plant materials.

Dogwood blossoms are very delicate so do not handle them more than is absolutely necessary. Hold the flowers up against the arrangement or gently set them in among the other plant materials to be sure you know where they are to go before wiring them. The two small blossoms at the top should be about two and one-half inches below the tallest leaf. Six go just above the pitcher's rim, and three make a middle row. All of these are pushed in farther than the brunia. With water-soluble glue, attach one flower to the lid.

Place three 'Navajo' zinnias around the center top of the bouquet, but one and one-half inches below the top leaf. Zig-zag seven around the bottom and five around the middle.

Again, hold the arrangement at eye level to see whether any of the bouquet's structure shows. If necessary, add more leaves or brunia.

Inventory of Dried Plant Materials

This inventory is provided for the identification and preparation of plant materials used in the dried arrangements described in this book. The horticultural names of those plants collected or cultivated in the United States are given; the names commonly used on the market are provided for readily available imports and other plant materials that are usually purchased rather than grown by flower arrangers. The catalogs of seedsmen, plantsmen, and suppliers of dried materials will also be helpful in the growing or collecting of flowers, leaves, pods, and cones for winter bouquets.

ALBIZZIA POD
Albizzia julibrissin

Beautiful long green pods with visible seeds grow in clusters on mimosa-like trees. In August, pick the clusters from the tree or collect newly fallen ones from the ground. Dry the whole cluster as flat as possible in silica gel for one week. Store-flat in a large tin with a little gel.

AMARANTH, GLOBE
Gomphrena globosa

Clover-like flowers in orange, cream (called white by most dealers), pink, and rose-purple are easy to cultivate. Pick the blossoms all summer to keep the plants from going to seed and hang dry. Wire into clusters or spikes.

ARTEMISIA 'SILVER KING'
Artemisia albula

Silvery gray leaves and stems must be gathered before the yellow flowers appear or after the seed head has formed. Pick two-foot pieces and hang dry for straight stems. For natural curves, place stems in a container with a little water and leave until the water has evaporated and stems and leaves are dry. Use whole stem or wire into spikes.

BABY'S BREATH
Gypsophila paniculata

Small and white papery flowers grow on much branched stems of perennial plants. Hang dry until the moisture has been removed from the stems. Before using in arrangements, place the branches in a plastic bag and sprinkle them with warm water. Seal the bag and allow to stand for several hours or overnight. Break into manageable pieces for arrangements. Often used as fill.

BACHELOR'S BUTTON *Centaurea cyanus*

Annual flowers are available in blue, purple, pink and white, but the brilliant blue one is the most treasured by dried flower arrangers. Dry, face down, in silica gel with one-inch stems for two or three days. Often used as focal points.

BEARD-TONGUE, HAIRY *Penstemon hirsutus*

Clusters of small and attractive brown seed pods are borne on tall branched stems. Hang dry and coat with clear florist spray. Use natural stems for large arrangements and wire the side branches of pods for small bouquets.

BEECH LEAVES *Fagus grandifolia*

Preserve large sprays of these graceful, many-veined leaves either by pressing them between several layers of newspaper or by treating them with glycerine and water. Pick just after the new growth has hardened or the leaves will curl. When pressing leaves, arrange them so they do not touch each other, and allow them to remain in the paper until you need them.

Glycerine-treated leaves turn dark green and then brown, depending on the time they are left in the solution. Remove them when they look the way you want them to, air dry for a few days, and then store in a cardboard box with tissue paper.

BLACK-EYED SUSAN *Rudbeckia hirta*

These lovely yellow or gold daisies with dark centers are ancestors of the more frequently cultivated gloriosa daisy. They may be cultivated, but are usually collected from the wild. Dry, face down, in silica gel for three to seven days. Wire as single flowers and use as focal points.

BLOODWORT *Lachnanthes tinctoria*
RED ROOT

This beige-gray perennial grows near swamps and cranberry bogs. It has a soft and velvety finish and is branched at the top of a thin stem where dull yellow flowers appear. Pick after seeds have formed and hang dry. Use primarily for fill on natural stems.

BOXWOOD LEAVES *Buxus sempervirens*

This handsome evergreen has branches of shiny green leaves. It is slow growing, but save whatever prunings you can find for the base of arrangements and for hiding the Oasis in more open bouquets. Press the branches in newsprint or treat them in a glycerine solution. They do not have to be wired. The wide and flat branches are most useful.

BRUNIA FRUIT Import

Sprays of fruits that look like small gray golf balls appear on coarse rope-like branches. They are imported from Africa and are available from commercial suppliers. Wire as natural sprays for woodsy arrangements.

BUTTON, FLORAL   Import

These compact round heads are some of the most common plant materials found on the dried flower market. They are available in several sizes and many are dyed in brilliant colors. You will have to shop to find them in their natural off-white. You might find some equivalents growing near ponds; other kinds are the centers of daisy-like flowers. They are usually wired into spikes.

CALENDULA   *Calendula officinalis*

This easy to cultivate annual bears large yellow or orange ray flowers all season. Dry, face down, in silica gel from three to seven days. Frequently wired singly and used as focal points.

CELOSIA, PLUME   *Celosia plumosa*

Heavy and hardy spikes of feathery side shoots in shades of gold and red are abundant on this easily cultivated annual. They both dry darker. Pick early and hang dry in bunches of no more than six stalks for at least two weeks. Clean the stem below the plume by rubbing it, and break off the more delicate side shoots to wire into spikes. The remaining center of the natural bloom makes a heavier spike.

CHINESE LANTERN   *Physalis alkekengi francheti*

These bright orange pods are grown on hardy perennial plants that are likely to crowd out other plants unless they are contained. Pick the stiff stems of lanterns as the pods are starting to turn orange and also later when they have already reached their most brilliant color. Hang dry for straight stems or dry in a container for curves.

The lanterns can be turned into flowers by cutting along their veins. See the instructions for the Chinese lantern arrangement.

The fragile pods often fall from their stems, but they can be glued back on. All can be made secure by running a little Duco cement down the dried stem and around the base of the lantern.

CHIVE, ORIENTAL   *Allium tuberosum*

A burst of white star-like flowers appears atop a tall stem on this self seeding plant. Pick the clusters before all the buds have opened and dry them, face down, in silica gel for at least two weeks. Dry separate long stems on their sides in the same tin. These can be used to lengthen the natural stems for open arrangements. The odor left in the gel will disappear after it has been sifted and baked.

CINQUEFOIL, ROUGH-FRUITED   *Potentilla recta*

The soft green of the toothed and hairy leaves and unopened buds provide one of the best greens for dried arrangements. Cultivate from seed or division or pick from the wild before the plant branches and flowers. Hang dry and wire in clusters of two or three stems.

COCKSCOMB   *Celosia argentea cristata*

Velvety heads of red and gold cockscomb are the long lasting products of annual plants. The crests vary in shade with different soils, with age, and with the drying process to produce a variety of pinks, rusts, reds, golds, and beiges. Hang dry for two weeks. The large crests are too heavy for most arrangements, but they can be broken into small clusters and wired for maneuverability. Always clean the stem just below the crest by rubbing it, and have the colorful head facing in an appropriate direction.

COTTON POD   *Gossypium* varieties

The opened pods of some varieties of cotton look like star-shaped flowers that have an irridescent inner surface and a dark brown outer one. Pods are dry by the time the cotton has been removed. Wire two or three together in a cluster for woodsy arrangements. Several varieties are available on the market, but try some field grown ones if you can find them.

DAISY, AFRICAN   *Helipterum roseum*
ACROLINIUM

Yellow, pink, and white blossoms resemble strawflowers, but are more irridescent, less double, and more delicate. Quantities of these blossoms are imported from Africa and are available on the market, even though they can be cultivated here. Pick buds and just opening flowers and hang dry until all moisture has been removed from the soft and woolly stems. Before wiring the fragile flowers, cut the stem to about one inch and run Duco cement down the stem and around the base of the flower. Dried buds can be opened with your fingers.

DAISY, ENGLISH   *Bellis perennis*

Single, usually white, ray flowers are borne on perennial plants in spring and summer. Pick before the central disk has fully opened and dry in silica gel, face up or down, with enough stem for wiring. Run glue down the short stem and around the base of the blossom, especially where the petals are attached. Wire singly and use as focal points.

DAISY, SHASTA   *Chrysanthemum maximum*

These large white ray flowers are borne on perennial plants in summer. Gel dry for three to seven days, face up or down, with enough stem to wire. Run Duco cement down the short stem and around the base of the flower, especially where petals are attached. Wire singly and use for focal points.

                                          Chrysanthemum coronarium
DAISY, YELLOW   *C. frutescens*

Yellow daisies are easy to grow annuals and perennials. Pick the blossoms early and dry, face up or face down, in silica gel. Run a little Duco cement down the short stem and around the base of the flower, especially where the petals are attached. If a petal falls off dip it in the cement and put it back in place. Daisies are usually wired singly and used as focal points.

DELPHINIUM   *Delphinium* varieties

Tall spikes of mostly blue flowers appear in June and July and are invaluable for dried arrangements. Dry the tips of the spikes on their sides and individual side blossoms face up on a hill of gel. The tip of the long spire can be wired and used as a spike and the lower side flowers can be wired singly and used as focal points. Light blue blossoms tend to fade to almost white when dried in silica gel, but the dark or electric blue varieties retain their color well.

DOCK   *Rumex* varieties

The tall stalks of this "weed" are one of the dried flower arranger's most useful plant materials. Pick from the field in three stages for first green, then pink-beige, and finally rusty brown to almost black spikes. Be sure to make the first cutting after the long branched head has filled out but is still green. This stage lasts for about two weeks; the pinkish cast lasts for only one week. Hang dry. The whole spike might be used for massive arrangements, but usually the side shoots are removed and wired into small spikes.

DOGWOOD   *Cornus florida*

Dogwood trees are protected in most states, so you can pick blossoms only from trees on your own or a friend's land. Pick the lovely white flowers in the early spring before the green center has opened. Try also to collect some tiny blossoms and young ones that have a greenish cast. Dry all of these, face down in silica gel. It is sometimes difficult to wire the blossoms because they have such tiny stems. If necessary, they can be glued into arrangements, where they are often used for focal points.

Sprays of dogwood leaves can be pressed in newspaper or treated with a glycerine solution.

EVERLASTING, AFRICAN   Import

This imported dried flower is irridescent and stark white with a white center. It grows on a soft and fuzzy stem. Break off all but one inch of the stem and wire as a single blossom or a blossom and a bud.

EVERLASTING, PEARLY   *Anaphalis margaritacea*

The loose clusters of small white flowers with green centers can be found along the roadsides and in uncultivated fields in late summer. Pick them early for the blossoms will continue to develop as they dry and the center will become fuzzy. Hang dry. Break the small clusters from the large head and wire into smaller and more compact clusters or into spikes.

FERNS

Many ferns are valuable in dried bouquets for their green color and for their light and airy texture. They can be pressed in several layers of newspaper and pressed under weights or they can be dried in silica gel. The color is retained better by silica gel. Fertile leaves can be hang dried or purchased from dried flower suppliers. The four ferns used in these arrangements are the leather fern (*Rumorha adianiformis*), maidenhair (*Adiantum pedatum*), and narrow-leaved chain-fern (*Woodwardia areolata*). The long leaves of leather fern are rather heavy and dark green; the broad leaves of the maidenhair are branched into two or three segments and are quite delicate. The chain-fern has large pinnate leaves, and the fertile leaf of sensitive fern is covered with small beads. Experiment with your own plants and the leaves available from florist shops.

FEVERFEW   *Chrysanthemum parthenium*

Sprays of small white daisy-like flowers appear on perennial plants in June and into summer. Pick especially the sprays of early blossoms and dry them horizontally in silica gel. Wire as a natural spray.

FREESIA   *Freesia refracta*

The fragrant flowers have raceme-like spikes at right angles to the stems. They may be grown from bulbs and forced indoors. Dry each spike with one inch of stem on its side in silica gel for about one week. The spikes can be wired or the natural stem can be inserted in a Queen Anne's lace stem for more open arrangements.

GAS PLANT   *Dictamnus albus*

The green pods of this perennial are star shaped and grow on tall stalks with infrequent side shoots. The stalks can be hang dried and the side shoots wired into spikes.

GLOBE THISTLE   *Echinops ritro*

These bold and prickly thistles have a silvery blue color and provide a good change in texture for heavier arrangements. Cultivate or pick from the wild before the plant blooms. Hang dry the stalks and wire the thistles singly.

GOLDENROD   *Solidago* varieties

This underestimated "weed" has branched stalks of small yellow flowers. Pick the stalks in late July and early August. Select those blossoms that have not fully opened, for the flowers will continue to develop as they dry and will become fuzzy. Hang dry the stalks, which can be used in large arrangements. For most bouquets and for graceful curves, break off the side shoots and wire them into spikes.

There are over one hundred varieties of goldenrod.

GRAINS AND GRASSES

Many dried grasses and grains are available on the market, can be picked from the fields, or may be grown as ornamentals. The black grass used here is imported from Hawaii. It is dark brown and looks a little like a very open and elongated grain head. Lagurus (*Lagurus ovatus*), also known as hares-tail-grass and rabbit-tail-grass, is an ornamental with wooly tufts that are well described by their common names. Pampas grass (*Cortaderia selloana*) is a very tall ornamental with a large plume. Plume grass or erianthus (*Erianthus revennae*) is another tall ornamental with a very large and airy plume. Sea grass (*Ammophila breviligulata*) has a long and dense spike or seed head.

Wheat (*Triticum*) and millet (*Panicum*) both have rather short spikes of seeds—the wheat spike is separated with distinct seeds; the millet head is tight, dense, and narrow.

HYDRANGEA   *Hydrangea species and varieties*

These flower clusters change color as they mature and some kinds change with the degree of soil acidity. White, blue, green, and pink blossoms are available from the different sorts in their various stages and settings. Pick them in all stages and all colors, especially before all the buds have opened. Hang-dried hydrangea curls more than gel-dried flowers. Break into small clusters with short stems and place them on their sides in silica gel. Wire as natural clusters.

IMMORTELLE   Import

These loose clusters of small yellow flowers are hardy and hold their color well. They are natives of Italy, Spain, and France and are readily available on the market, sometimes bleached or dyed. Break off individual blossoms or small clusters and wire into either tight clusters or spikes.

LAMB'S EAR   *Stachys lanata*

The leaves and stems of this hardy perennial are gray and covered with white hair. Disbud before the purple flowers appear, and hang dry.

LARKSPUR   *Delphinium ajacis*

This annual dephinium has attractive spikes of pink, purple, blue, and white flowers. Pick the long stalks before the top buds have opened and hang dry. Later in the season side shoots develop. Dry these in silica gel since they are small enough to fit into containers. All are used as natural spikes on their natural stems or wired. The white blossoms dry better than most white flowers.

LAUREL, LEAVES   *Kalmia latifolia*

Sprays of these elongated and shiny leaves develop a coppery tone and then become dark brown when placed in a solution of glycerine and water. Pick the sprays while the sap is running and place them in a solution of glycerine and water. Remove the leaves when they have turned the color you are looking for. Dry the stems with paper towels and allow the sprays to dry in the air for a few days before storing them in cardboard boxes with tissue paper. Use the natural stems or wire the sprays for full arrangements.

LOOSESTRIFE, PURPLE   *Lythrum salicaria*

The tall spikes of reddish purple flowers grow in fields and along the roadsides. Pick before the top buds have opened and hang dry for dark purple spikes. Use the natural stem or wire.

MAGNOLIA   *Magnolia grandiflora*

The large and shiny green leaves of the southern magnolia tree become soft and pliable and turn brown to almost black when they are treated with glycerine and water. The darker shades produced by more time in the solution are usually used in traditional arrangements. Allow heavy or double wires to go halfway up the back of the leaf to help support it. Dried flower suppliers often carry these leaves, sometimes already wired.

MARIGOLD
Tagetes varieties

All but the small button forms of these yellow and gold annuals dry well in silica gel. Put the single blossoms in the drying container face down, the others face up. Wire individual blossoms in the usual manner for single flowers or put a little tape on the end of a floral wire, dip it in glue, and then insert it in the hollow stem.

MONEY
HONESTY
Lunaria annua

Money is an easily cultivated and self-seeding plant whose tall stalks bear many side branches of flat and circular seed-pods in late summer and early fall. Cut the stalks when the pods are dry and hang until the moisture has left the stalks. With your thumb and forefinger, rub each pod to remove the outer coverings and the seeds, revealing the silvery and transparent coins. The tall stalks can be used, but wired side shoots are better for most arrangements.

OKRA
Hibiscus esculentus

Interesting curves make these long and ribbed pods of the southern vegetable very dramatic in woodsy arrangements. When they are mature, they are naturally in shades of beige, but it is also possible to purchase bleached pods which are almost white and particularly effective. Use double wires and wire the pods singly.

PEONY
Paeony varieties

The large and handsome flowers of these perennials are dramatic in massive arrangements and the opening buds look a bit like roses. The red blossoms dry darker, but the pink and white ones hold their colors well. Pick in several stages with one and one-half inch stems. Dry the flowers, main buds, and leaves in silica gel. Place the blossoms in the container face up, the buds on their sides, and the leaves flat. Single flowers dry in about one week, but the buds may take up to three weeks. Peony leaves are a much underestimated green for both fresh and dried arrangements.

PEPPER BERRIES
Schinus molle

Clusters of rose colored berries are the fruits of a weeping evergreen tree that grows in South America and California. They are hang dried and are available on the market. When small clusters are wired into elongated clusters, they look like gracefully drooping racemes. Clear florist spray gives them an attractive sheen.

PETTICOAT LACE
INDIAN PETTICOAT   *Oxytheca perfoliata*
PUNCTURED BRACT

This pink desert annual has saucer-like bracts on thin and branched stems.
It can be picked from the high plains of the Southwest or purchased from
commercial sources. After it has dried in the air, break off the sprays and
wire them as you would a natural cluster, but be careful of the thorns. Clear
spray changes the color to orange.

PINE CONE   *Pinus* varieties

Cones of pines in many sizes and shapes can be picked up from the ground
below trees in late summer and fall. Many varieties are also available on
the market. Wire the large ones singly and the small ones in clusters for
woodsy arrangements.

PUSSY WILLOW   *Salix discolor*

The stems of pussy willows make good false stems for flowers, like roses,
with naturally dark stems. They can be air-dried in a vase or by hanging.

QUEEN ANNE'S LACE   *Daucus carota*

Delicate white flower heads grow in the fields and along the roadsides all
over the United States. Dry face down in silica gel for from five to seven
days. Be sure to dry extra stems in the same tin. These are used for false
stems for flowers in light and airy arrangements.

ROSE   *Rosa* varieties

Experiment with your roses and with hot house blossoms from the florist
shops. Dry them with one inch stems, face up, on hills of silica gel. Dry
buds that are not too tight on their sides and leaf sprays spread flat. Single
roses will dry in two or three days; fuller blossoms and buds will naturally
take longer. Put Duco cement around the base of the flower after it has
dried. Pink roses maintain their color better than the others. White blossoms often turn cream, yellow flowers fade, and red ones become dark,
sometimes almost black.

SALVIA, BLUE   *Salvia farinacea*

This tender perennial which is grown as an annual, is easy to cultivate and
bears small spikes of blue flowers that dry well. Pick before the blossoms at
the tip of the spike have opened and hang dry. Two or three natural spikes
are usually wired into a spike. Red salvia does not dry well.

SNAPDRAGON   *Antirrhinum majus*

Spikes of rose, purple, yellow, and white flowers are borne on easily cultivated annual plants in mid-summer. Pick before all the buds have opened
and dry on their sides in silica gel. Wire and use as natural spikes.

SPIREA   *Spiraea billiardi*

Deciduous shrubs bear dense panicles of small pink flowers in mid-summer. Pick before all buds have opened and dry on their sides in silica gel. Wire as a natural cluster.

SPIREA, LEAVES   *Spiraea prunifolia*

Long branches of simple and alternate leaves turn a kind of metallic green when treated with glycerine and water. Branches of many lengths can be cut from the tips of the branches for large and small bouquets. Use either the natural stems or wires.

STARFLOWER   Import

Starflowers are readily available on the market in a multitude of colors. The small and delicate blossoms have long and very fine stems so they can easily be wired into long spikes for open or stuffed arrangements. Many are imported from Brazil.

STATICE, DOMESTIC   *Limonium sinuatum*

Hardy annual or biennial plants bear elongated clusters of papery flowers in white, pink, yellow, lavender, and purple. These are popular commercial products, but they can be cultivated easily. Hang dry.

STATICE, GERMAN   Import

Most German statice used here is imported, although it can be grown along the sea coasts in the United States. Since it takes a lot of space, buying it is more economical. Before using the stiff branches of hang dried white flowers, place them in a plastic bag and sprinkle them with a little warm water as you would clothes to be ironed. Allow them to stand for several hours, but no more than twenty-four, so they can be more easily managed. German statice is frequently used as fill and is sometimes wired into spikes.

STRAWFLOWERS   *Helichrysum* varieties

These commercially popular flowers in mostly yellow and gold have been improved by hybridization and are now available in red, pink, and white. If you grow them yourself, pick the blossoms before the center has opened. Remove the natural stem and insert a wire into the base of the flower, but do not push it through so far that it will be visible from the blossom's face. Place the wired flowers in a container. They tighten around the wire as they dry. Strawflowers sold on the market usually have very flimsy wires. Treat these the way you would treat natural stems and attach wires of floral weight. Wire large strawflowers singly or with a bud and the small ones as spikes.

TANSY   *Tanacetum vulgare*

This branched perennial can be cultivated or found in the wild. It bears small button-like flowers that must be picked when they are bright yellow and not after they have started to darken. Hang dry the stalks and wire the small buttons into spikes.

WOOD ROSE   Import

These pods are produced on tropical vines that are relatives of the morning glory. They are perfectly described by their name. Some are large single roses and others are smaller and grow in clusters. Most are imported from Hawaii. Wire them for accents in woodsy arrangements.

YARROW, YELLOW   *Achillea ageratum*

Dense heads of tiny yellow flowers grow on hardy perennial plants in summer and into autumn. Pick when the flowers are open but before they have been damaged by rain or insects and hang dry. Small natural heads can be wired and used as clusters. Pieces can be broken from larger heads and wired into clusters.

ZINNIA   *Zinnia* varieties

Easily propagated annual plants bear blossoms in many sizes, shapes, and colors. All dry well in silica gel, but the smaller single ones are most useful in dried arrangements. Dry them, face down, in silica gel and wire them singly for focal points. Experiment with many of these hardy blossoms.